The Man Who Launched a Thousand Poems
Volume One

Selected works

For adults:
Fighting Talk: A COVID-19 Poetry Diary, Vol. 1 †
Can of Worms: A COVID-19 Poetry Diary, Vol. 2 †
Pig's Ear, Dg's Dinner: A COVID-19 Poetry Diary, Vol. 3 †
Nail on the Head: A COVID-19 Poetry Diary, Vol. 4 †
The Man Who Launched a Thousand Poems, Vol. 1 †
The Man Who Launched a Thousand Poems, Vol. 2 †

Touched by The Band of Nod – The Slade Poems •
The Saturday Men •

For children:
Football 4 Every 1 ★
The Very Best of Paul Cookson ★
Paul Cookson's Joke Shop ★
There's a Crocodile in the House ✦

As Editor:
The Works ★
100 Brilliant Poems for Children ★
Fire Burn, Cauldron Bubble ▲

† Published by Flapjack Press
• Published by A Twist in the Tale & available at paulcooksonpoet.co.uk
★ Published by Pan Macmillan ✦ Published by Otter Barry Books
▲ Published by Bloomsbury

PAUL COOKSON

THE MAN WHO LAUNCHED A THOUSAND POEMS

VOLUME ONE

Illustrated by Martin Chatterton

Flapjack Press

flapjackpress.co.uk
Exploring the synergy between performance and the page

Published in 2023 by Flapjack Press
Salford, Gtr Manchester
⊕ flapjackpress.co.uk ▶ Flapjack Press
f Flapjack Press 🐦 FlapjackPress

ISBN 978-1-7396231-8-0

Cover & illustrations by Martin Chatterton
⊕ worldofchatterton.com 📷 edchatt

Author photo by Sally Cookson

Poems 1–114 were first published in *Fighting Talk*,
115–223 in *Can of Worms*, 224–392 in *Pig's Ear, Dog's Dinner*,
and 393–500 in *Nail on the Head*.

Printed by Imprint Digital
Upton Pyne, Exeter, Devon
⊕ digital.imprint.co.uk

FSC

MAN
CHE
STER

A UNESCO City
of Literature

*Dedicated to Henry Normal –
long-time friend, fellow poet,
and all-round good fellow.*

Contents

Introduction

Lockdown seems a long time ago now but things did literally change overnight. My work as a poet in schools stopped. I suddenly had nowhere to go and nothing to do on a daily basis. Like so many others.

But with adversity and change comes time and opportunity. Partly inspired by Chris Riddell and his daily cartoon, I started to write a daily poem and put it out on various social media outlets – Facebook, Twitter, Instagram.

It was always in the morning and began as my own personal response to what was happening. I started – and have never stopped. At first, I thought it would just be while we had COVID and lockdown – thinking it would be a month or two. But then, inspired by the online responses and comments I carried on. And on. And on ...

One audience had been replaced with another. Virtual applause, immediate reactions. Encouragement and purpose.

Unwittingly, I had redefined myself. Not just a poet for children but a writer for adults, too.

And then came Paul and Flapjack Press. Long-time friend and fellow poet, Henry Normal suggested I contact Paul as his collections had been published with Flapjack.

I'll be honest – it was probably the shortest email I'd ever sent to a potential publisher. It was on the Thursday morning before Father's Day – I wasn't expecting a reply but got one Thursday afternoon. The Monday after Father's Day, Paul agreed to publish *Fighting Talk*. Then *Can of Worms*. Then *Pig's Ear, Dog's Dinner*. Then *Nail on the Head*. And then this ... these.

And so it began ... and here we are. And it is "we".

Thank you, everyone

Paul Cookson
January 2023

The Man Who Launched a Thousand Poems
Volume One

The Day The World Stood Still
#1 / 23:03:2020

More than just – trouble at t'mill
More than flu to make you ill
More than a virus – it will kill
The day the world stood still

No quick fix, no magic pill
Vaccination numbers – nil
Feel the fear, fear the chill
The day the world stood still

Now we've too much time to fill
Going to be a long, long time until
We do those things we know we will
The day the world stood still

This is the day
This is the day
This the day world stood

But I'm Not
#2 / 24:03:2020

Today, I should have been
At a school in Stoke-on-Trent
But I'm not

Right now, I should be mid-performance
Laughter and audience participation echoing
Like pantomime – but with better rhymes
But I'm not

I'm here, home
With a cup of tea and biscuits
A brand new notebook and pen
And this poem
Which I wouldn't usually be writing

Small part of me – glad of the time here
Not too busy to take a breath
Have another cup of tea
And another biscuit – of course
But the rest of me
Worried

Really worried
Anxious about the crossings out
The cancellations in my diary
The immediate disappearance of work
And the uncertainty

What To Do With All This Time?
#3 / 25:03:2020

I suppose that I've always wanted
Much more time to write
But now that it's real and here
It doesn't feel quite right

   And that can't be a rhyme
   Just because it's spelt differently
   It still sounds like the same word
   So I've failed already ...

I could finish the novel I long-ago started
Complaining I never had the time
Go through all my files and notebooks
Unfinished poems, forgotten good lines

Sort out all the ideas and plans
The seeds that have fallen along the way
I bought a brand new notebook so maybe
I could even write a new poem every day ...

Connection
#4 / 26:03:2020

Doors open – we pause
And then – applause
That ripple effect
As isolates connect
A standing ovation
Appreciation

This strange communion
Our separate union
A simple act of hope
Together we vote
NHS
Quite simply – yes

[23]

Now Is The Time
#5 / 27:03:2020

Now is not the time to be cynical
More a time to be ecumenical

It isn't right, the centre or the left
It's trying to work out just what is the best

A crisis that is bringing us together
A virus that is changing us forever

But in this crisis let us recall
Those who did not value this at all

Those who thought that value was financial
Highest bidders, markets and potential

Private money-makers from elsewhere
Profit before people, cash before healthcare

If and when – eventually – those of us get through
Let us learn right now a value that is true

Cherish and protect at any cost
This jewel in our crown must not be lost

Safeguard doctors, nurses, safeguard health
For future generations – that's true wealth

"Great work." *Keith Baxter*

Like Any Other Day
#6 / 28:03:2020

It could be like any other day
The house is quiet
The first cup of tea tastes good
And the birds outside still sing of heaven

It could be like any other day
I'm thinking of toast
Butter, marmalade – hey, even both
I can hear a clock ticking – or is it the fridge?

It could be like any other day
The TV is quiet
News is not news yet
Reality still slumbers, daydreaming

The sun still shines
Majestic as it ever did
Just like any other day
But it isn't

Heartache, worry, anxiety
Will soon overwhelm us
But for now, the house is quiet
And it could be like any other day

And On The Seventh Day ...
#7 / 29:03:2020

Sunday used to be
            A day of rest
Now it's just another day
            Like all the rest
Sunday used to be
            The only day we'd pray
Now some of us are praying
            Every single day

This Is The New Normal
#8 / 30:03:2020

This is the new normal
But if it isn't
More time to read and talk
Watch and listen
Socialise online
Isolate together in small groups and spaces
In this new normal
That is anything
But

This is the new normal
Baked potatoes
Toilet roll rationing
Hand gel wars
Empty streets and parks
Closed pub doors
In this new normal
That is anything
But

This is the new normal
Experimental baking
Online front room fitness routines
Cleaning out the garden shed
And writing poems like this
In this new normal
That is anything
But

This is the new normal
But it isn't
The same arguments fester
The same disagreements jar
The petty and the life changing
Or the "just getting on each other's nerves"
All confined
All magnified
In this new normal
That is anything
But

Oh ... The Irony
#9 / 31:03:2020

Ironically
With more time on my hands
I've elected not to shave
And therefore grow a beard
For the duration
Thus giving me extra time
To write poems like this

Pardon?
What's that you say?

Start shaving again ...

Haiku
#10 / 01:04:2020

The first of April
The fool still rules and we all
Wish it was fake news

April The Second
#11 / 02:04:2020

It's April the second
And the joke isn't over
Usually by now
It's the big reveal …
Ha ha! April Fool!

Spaghetti on trees
Water in tablets
The Loch Ness Monster
Tartan paint

Not this year
Not this time

It's April the second
Hospitals under increasing pressure
Lockdown, no jobs
More deaths every day
Friends and family affected

How we long for a stupid
Harmless April Fool
Instead we have this
April that is cruel

Still
#12 / 03:04:2020

I found my watch today
Unworn
Stopped
Nine fifty-five
Morning or evening ...
Who knows – or cares?
Time has stood still

The diary – last used three weeks ago
Days of work now cancelled
Irrelevant, unused, redundant
For the foreseeable
Time has stood still

I have no use for such as these
Unnecessary at present
Right now
As there is only "the right now"
Seconds, minutes, hours,
Days, weeks, months
They are all just ... now

Time stands still
Time stands still
Time stands still
Time stands
Time stands
Time stands
Till it is time to move on

The Worst
#13 / 04:04:2020

Today was a difficult day
Quiet, eerie, solemn, edgy

Missing loved ones
Elderly parents, brothers, sisters …
Especially the children

Not children anymore
But still our babies
The house seems even quieter
Mostly that's been good, but even so …

As viral thoughts swirl viciously
Thinking the worst

The worst is starting to happen
The worst will happen to someone we know
Probably sometime soon now

And here we are
Hoping that it doesn't happen to us
But if that's the best we can hope for
Can we really call that hope?

"Part of my daily landscape." *Jen Tyler-Stevens*

Sunshine And A Sunny Day
#14 / 05:04:2020

Sunshine and a sunny day
And it's easy to say
That things are better, everything's okay
But it's not

Sunshine and a sunny day
It's got to be good to enjoy the weather
Be together anyway
But it's not

Sunshine and a sunny day
Outside it's nice – let's ignore advice
Whatever some may say
But we can't

Sunshine and a sunny day
Surely that nullifies the threat of death
That just won't go away
But it doesn't

Selfishness, ignorance, stupidity
Unaffected by the weather and humanity
Facts remain the same
Inside you should stay
Even when there's sunshine and a sunny day

A Cup Of Tea And A Good Night's Sleep
#15 / 06:04:2020

When I was young
Mum would always say
A cup of tea and a good night's sleep
And everything will be okay

Sickness, bumps, every ache
A little bit of flu
And right now
I wish that this was true

Viral
#16 / 07:04:2020

It does not discriminate
Everyone is equal
This deadly evil predator
Spreads misery and death to all

Old, young, male, female
Rich, poor, black, white, far and wide
A bus driver or a Prime Minister

Compassion is the same
It must be viral
We cannot choose those we wish well

Our hearts must reach to everyone
And if we cannot do that
We do not have compassion

And have no heart at all

I Will Not Clap For Boris
#17 / 08:04:2020

I will not clap for Boris
Although I wish him well
And when he has recovered
Perhaps he'll have discovered
The NHS
Is just the best
And not something to sell

I Was Late To The Party – But You'd Already Left

#18 / 09:04:2020
for John Prine

Too many records and too little time
Folks kept telling me 'bout John Prine
If you like good songs – well he's one of the best
I was late to the party – but you'd already left

Was it just another voice, just another guitar
Just another country rock and roll star?
Well I was wrong – I must confess
I was late to the party – but you'd already left

Nothing that special? Nothing that new?
But it was so different because it was you
Humanity in every single breath
I was late to the party – but you'd already left

A song and a story and a smile on your face
You took us on the road to a different place
Heaven is somewhere – way out west
I was late to the party – but you'd already left

Humility in each melody
A living, breathing legacy
Once I was ignorant – now I say yes
I was late to the party – but you'd already left

Summer's at an end – before it's begun
God's own singer – God's own songs
Teach 'em to the angels – they can join with the rest
I was late to the party – but you'd already left

Not Walking Alone
#19 / 10:04:2020

Last night, my evening walk took me
Through fields and stiles and stiles and fields

The route I used to walk
With our beloved Springer Spaniel

Only now, I walk to the canal
Never with Max – he'd be in like a shot

I'd forgotten about the eight o'clock clap
So found myself mid-meadow

Applauding
Thinking I would be alone

Yet, echoing in the distance
I heard the ripple of spreading applause

Shouts, cheers – and even a stereo
Playing Gerry and the Pacemakers

And for someone who was walking alone
I was not

"Fantastic." *Garry Clarkson*

Silver Linings
#20 / 11:04:2020

The blossom seems pinker
The grass is much greener
The sunshine seems warmer
Atmosphere – cleaner

Evenings are longer
Mornings seem lighter
Daffodils yellower
Snowdrops much whiter

The sky is much bluer
Birdsong is clearer
Silence is golden
Heaven is nearer

Easter Sunday: One
#21 / 12:04:2020

Friday was in no way "Good"
Nine hundred and eighty dead
Saturday – nine hundred and seventeen

So – on Easter Sunday
When we should be thinking of
Resurrection, hope, new life

We just can't help but fear the worst

Easter Sunday: Two – Haiku
#22 / 12:04:2020

On Easter Sunday
We celebrate an empty
Tomb – but not today

An Oldie But A Goodie
#23 / 13:04:2020
for Tim Brooke Taylor

When I was young
I wanted to be Bill most of all
Long haired, funny and flared
The daft one, the wannabe rock star

Then Graeme
Corduroy boffin, brains and wit
Exotic spelling

I always thought Timbo
The wet one, the weak one
The one who didn't write the jokes

Not just an equal third
Not just a vital cog
Not just a teapot impression and Union Jack waistcoat

But a writer, performer
Funny – really funny
In his own write
I'm sorry – I just hadn't a clue

Yorkshiremen and undercover police
Nearly a Python
You ended up more than a Goodie
Smut never sounded smutty with you

You read it again
You had more than a clue
Tim Brooke Taylor
Thank you

Named
#24 / 14:04:2020

That's the lot of you – named
Hang your heads – you should be ashamed
Your actions – they should be explained
Rejecting the pay that the nurses had claimed

You cheered when their wages remained
Pitifully low, said money was strained
That a rise of this size could not be sustained
But bailing out banks is attained

Your reputations – all stained
Hospitals – broken and drained
Taking for granted all those who trained
To help the infirm, the ill and the pained

The whole sorry lot of you – named
The whole sorry lot of you – shamed
The whole sorry lot of you – blamed
… And the ten thousand pounds that you've gained

Covidiot
#25 / 15:04:2020

This ego – so mad and demented
These phrases and terms you've invented
The only new words
We wish we had heard
Is – Donald – you're – Un-President-Ed

Bad Rock Puns Warning ...
#26 / 16:04:2020

Feeling lock-*Down Down*
With COVID-19
Again and again
The same routine
Living on an Island
Would be a dream

We've got ...
Status Quo-rantine

Can You Hear Us Major Tom?
#27 / 17:04:2020

Captain Tom – yet your effort is major
Who would have thought
Walking round a garden a hundred times
Could capture the mood of a nation?

But it did – and it has
A heart-warming story in times of heartbreak
One hundred years old
And still able to walk around your garden

I suppose that's what you call
Ground Control, Major Tom
Your garden goal achieved
Target exceeded

You have promised to carry on
We applaud you
Can you hear us Major Tom?
Can you hear us Major Tom?

An example to us all
You have shown us where the true value lies
And who the heroes really are
We hear you Major Tom

Norman

#28 / 18:04:2020
for Norman Hunter

Even hard men cannot fight it
Even tough men cannot tackle it
You won most battles
Especially those on the pitch
Uncompromising, not one to be messed with
But not this one
Norman – you've been hunted

Your face on my Esso World Cup Coins
More than a name on a football card
Winner, champion
And alleged "biter of legs"
We may have called you dirty
But we'd have had you in our team
In a flash, our general
But, Norman – you have been hunted

More than just a hard man
More than just an enforcer
Vital cog in a winning team
Because of your reputation
Ability was overlooked
The skill and the steel
A real player's player

This time – unlike with Frannie Lee –
You could not fight back
This time
The opposition was too strong
And you lost
And just like many others lost
You are someone's son, husband
Father, granddad, loved one, friend ...

And they have lost too

Norman Hunter – one of a kind
Another good one gone

Cornflakes
#29 / 19:04:2020

This morning
I had Cornflakes for breakfast
At home – for the first time
In many a year

And it reminded me of
A thousand childhood breakfasts
Around a family kitchen table
Where we were allowed to add
A spoonful of sugar (only one, mind)

But mum and dad would never, ever
Ever buy Frosties

So – this morning
I had Cornflakes
With a spoonful – and a bit – of sugar
And, just for a few minutes
Life tasted a little bit sweeter

"Something to look forward to on a daily basis."
Harvinder Evans

Leaders Failing To Lead Us
#30 / 20:04:2020

It's coming to light that meetings were missed
COVID-19 – not top of your list
If this is true, the fact is just this
Leaders failing to lead us

Lessons not learned from countries elsewhere
Not taking note of what's happening there
Where is the diligence? Where is the care?
Leaders failing to lead us

It now seems that those in authority
Did not see this as a priority
The reality – for you and for me
Leaders failing to lead us

Underprepared – when warnings were clear
Blinkered and blasé – it can't happen here
Under-invested for many a year
Leaders failing to lead us

Not recognising a global pandemic
You don't have to be a great academic
But you are Dad's Army saying "Don't panic"
Leaders failing to lead us

Too little too late when lives are now lost
Too little too late – we're counting the cost
Too little too late – simply because
Leaders failing to lead us

It may have been "unpredictable" or
"Unprecedented" – but we can't ignore
You could have and should have done so much more
Leaders failing to lead us

Not A Good Time For My Business
#31 / 21:04:2020

Times they are hard, the times they are a-changing
The times that we live in are times that are strange in
My work possibilities need rearranging
Not a good time for my business

Pickings once rich – now they are nil
COVID-19 – with everyone ill
I cannot depend on public goodwill
Not a good time for my business

My night shifts have ended – left all alone
No-one gets out – they all stay at home
I cannot get in and take what you own
Not a good time for my business

Steeling myself for tough times ahead
Steeling myself – I'm now in the red
I'd steal from myself but there's nowt in my shed
Not a good time for my business

My livelihood has been taken away
I'd do the taking – but not today
Crime doesn't pay – true what they say
Not a good time for my business

No government help for someone like me
Usually me gets something for free
Not a good time for thieving and crime
Not a good time for my business

Nobody Famous Died Today
#32 / 22:04:2020

No beloved entertainer
Or footballer who used to play
No-one from the television
No-one famous died today

No singer of a favourite song
The one from all our yesterdays
No-one royal, no-one rich
No-one famous died today

Nurses, doctors, health workers
Front line folk on lower pay
Care assistants, helpers out
They're the ones who died today

Grandma Joan, Granddad Bill
Uncle Frank, Auntie May
A brother, sister, mum and dad
Important people died today

Someone special – every one
Taken – not just passed away
Those loved most – lost and gone
Too many that have died today

Too many every day

I Seem To Be Agreeing With Somebody Called Piers
#33 / 23:04:2020

These times are getting stranger – and stranger by the day
Where once I questioned everything that you would do and say
What's worrying and stranger still is now that it appears
I seem to be agreeing with somebody called Piers

Once smug and self-satisfied with ego so inflated
You almost seem respected where once you seemed so hated
A journalist investigates – after all these years!
I seem to be agreeing with somebody called Piers

Asking all the questions that are needing to be asked
PPE and testing and where are gowns and masks?
And why oh why the government is so far in arrears
I seem to be agreeing with somebody called Piers

That voice that was annoying seems now a people's voice
Shouting what we'd say if we had the means and choice
Raising our frustrations, empathising with our fears
I seem to be agreeing with somebody called Piers

Failures with mass gatherings and the need to be decisive
Hypocrisy and dithering – your questions now incisive
Who'd have thought that after all – you'd have such good ideas
I seem to be agreeing with somebody called Piers

Once I would be wishing you'd donate a vital organ
But now it's somewhat different with a different Mr Morgan
It's weird that we think you're great and do not grate our ears
I seem to be agreeing
Believing it is seeing
And despite your reputation
You are a human being
So I'll tip my hat, raise a glass and quietly say "cheers"
Blimey – I'm agreeing with somebody called Piers

Thank Our Lucky Stars
#34 / 24:04:2020

It's forever in the news 'coz we've got the lockdown blues
Dragging us down further – deeper in the dump
And while this virus is a curse, just think – it could be worse
We could be in America – with Trump

Pandemical deniers say the medicals are liars
And it's like a strain of flu or just like mumps
They ignore the facts of science and their sole reliance
Are the words and the actions of the Trumps

This land that's of the free riddled with stupidity
Re-open all the shops, fight the economic slump
Demanding liberty – ME – ME – ME
Just like the example of a certain Mr Trump

The president's suggestion is injection and digestion
Of disinfectant with a single pump
And salvation for the nation with UV radiation
The wisdom from the expert Dr Trump

Whose limited ideas have access to all ears
Loud enough to make you stop and jump
Ignores the scientific, cannot be specific
The general ignorance of Major Trump

Patriotic, idiotic, chronically psychotic
A despot who is spouting from his rump
Ignorance seems bliss – but the problem is
Lots of people listening to Trump

The future sure ain't bright – it's orange and it's shite
With this cranially challenged brainless chump
But the positive we've got is we're here and we're not
Living in America with Trump
Far beyond a joke that ordinary folk
Cannot see beyond this lard-ass lump
So thank our lucky stars that his government's not ours
And we are not misled by Donald Trump

Saturday Night Lockdown Blockbusters
#35 / 25:04:2020

Imagine what if
A boy with a quiff
A hero from Belgium that we know

Had a Reservoir Dog
Called Snowy because
It's ...

Tintin Quarantino

Priti Obvious, Priti Vacant
#36 / 26:04:2020

Shoplifting – at an all-time low
Tell us something we don't know

Football hooligans – they're down too
Burglaries – well, who knew?

Fewer car crashes this year
The M25 is nice and clear

Pretty clear that there's a link
Priti, please – stop and think

COVID-19 Killed The Radio Star ...
And Other Bad Pop Puns
(You have been warned ...)
#37 / 27:04:2020

Everybody Wants to Cure the World
Livin' on a Prayer at best
One Vaccination Under a Groove
With ...
Quaran-Tina Turner's Simply the Test

Overheard In A Supermarket Queue – Two Metres Apart
(He was talking loudly by the way)
#38 / 28:04:2020

Stay home
Stay safe
Two metres apart
Take note of the guidelines my dears

Social distancing ...
No problem
Me and the wife have done it for years

On The Passing Of Grandparents And Great Grandparents
#39 / 29:04:2020

Day by day by day by day
Silently, they slip away

Our ever-present everydays
Those constants in our family ways

No last goodbyes that we can say
No final prayers that we can pray

No favourite music we can play
One last time – our yesterdays

No holding hands, just where they lay
No hug, pretending it's okay

The distance that we have to stay
We cannot keep this force at bay

This lonely death, the price to pay
This generation – lost and grey

Day by day by day by day by day
Silently, they slip away

The Only Thing That's Doctored ...
#40 / 30:04:2020

A billion items – all supplied
To hospitals – nationwide
But the truth is more than this
And what's really happened is
Each individual item counts
To constitute these vast amounts
Camouflaged statistics while the problem's getting bigger
The only thing that's doctored are the figures

Count one single glove – not two
One single paper towel – it's true
One apron made from polythene
Not much to fight COVID-19
Not vital items – PPE
See this and you must agree
Ill-prepared, ill-thought out – a government that slumbers
The only thing that's doctored are the numbers

Pandemic warnings – all ignored
Stock not stockpiled, bought or stored
Can it be too much to ask
For simple things like gowns or masks?
If other governments could see
Potential problems why can't we?
Too late with too little while this virus still attacks
The only thing that's doctored are the facts

A government that we elect
Then has a duty to protect
A duty for decisive action
Not kneejerk copy-cat reaction
A duty then to plan and care
Due diligence to be prepared
For possible and probables and not remain aloof
The only thing that's doctored is the truth
These troubled times we live in are the proof
The only thing protected is the truth

At Least The Rain Will Keep The Idiots In
#41 / 01:05:2020

Hasn't it been lovely weather for this time of year?
But now the sunshine's gone and the drizzle's here
We live in hope that the sun will soon be back again
But at least the rain will keep the idiots in

Much too wet to walk that extra mile or two
Nowhere near dry enough for a barbecue
It's gone and put a dampener on family gatherings
But at least the rain will keep the idiots in

I'd rather see two or three putting up umbrellas
Than a bench with a bunch of chatting laughing fellas
Or a group of gossips, yapping, giggling
At least this rain will keep the idiots in

All this lockdown boredom is leading to resistance
Morons getting blasé about their social distance
If we ignore it all it's a battle we won't win
But at least the rain will keep the idiots in

There's calls for personal freedom and our civil rights
It's got to be for all of us – and even then it might …
Might just be that some of us live through COVID-19
But at least the rain will keep the idiots in

It's better that we don't get wetter
Follow guidelines to the letter
And if it has to rain all year then we'll take it on the chin
At least it keeps the idiots all in

The Satanic Versus ...
#42 / 02:05:2020

All the comings and the goings
Nothing that he isn't knowing
All the time his power growing
The dark lord sat in waiting
In the shadows at the back
Don't be fooled by his anorak
Dominic's on the attack
Like the power of Satan

Machiavellian puller of strings
Lurking, furtive in the wings
Plays the tune the puppet sings
Do not be mistaken
Sly and slimy, wily, weaselly
He'll hoodwink you oh so easily
Behind those glasses, scheming evilly
The darkened soul of Satan

Part hobgoblin, part dementor
Torturer and then tormentor
Herd mentality presenter
There is no escaping
From the one who's heard to say
If old ones die – then that's the way
The economy must be okay
The pawn that's born of Satan

Compassion, hope and empathy
Not in his vocabulary
All the herd mentality
Is the stance he's taken
Wouldn't touch him with a barge pole
Like to hit him with a large pole
Then chuck him down a really large hole
Bury him with Satan

The name that always comes up
When the Devil's mass debating
Demonic Comings – sums you up
You are ... the spawn of Satan

Solace
#43 / 03:05:2020
After listening to Chuck Prophet's 'Strings in the Temple'.

Today I didn't watch the news
Instead
I found solace in music
Strings sing and take me away
Cause goose-bumps to rise

Transported elsewhere
Real life forgotten in those moments
While notes transcend reality

Songs I knew and loved
Violins and strings
Love and hope in art
Solace in these things

Tomorrow – maybe a much-loved book
A painting, a psalm
A prayer, a poem
But these will give you solace
If we but give them time

"Thanks for keeping so many of us going." *Sue Wilson*

Hand In Hand
#44 / 04:05:2020

Once death has touched you
It holds you hand forever
Frozen fingers squeeze and squeeze
Until you are numb
Skeletal bones grind
Against the very skin of life itself
And while that life is ever-present
So, now, is that death
A circle, intertwined
Alpha, omega and all that lies between
Tight and cold right now
But it never lets you go
Time may loosen that grip
But forever now you are connected
Once death has touched you
It holds your hand forever

Fighting Talk
#45 / 05:05:2020

You cannot wrestle a virus
You cannot hit it back
A bug is not a mugger
With a random chance attack

You can't punch a pandemic
You cannot strangle a strain
You cannot grapple a germ
Retaliate vee pain

You cannot fight a battle
With a force that can't be seen
Fighting talk – useless words
Against COVID-19

Punk Rock Moustache

#46 / 06:05:2020
for Dave Greenfield

Punks didn't have moustaches
Punks didn't play the keyboards
But you were The Stranglers
And didn't care

Punks didn't have centre parting-ed longer hair
Punks didn't play longer songs
But you were The Stranglers
And didn't care

Punks didn't work with old jazz musicians
Or cover songs like 'Walk on By'
But you were The Stranglers
And didn't care

Moustaches and keyboards
Always more than a punk
You were the sound of The Stranglers
And we did care

Here To Stay Each Day
#47 / 07:05:2020

No-one grates your cheese greater
I'm your perfect toastie maker
Magic with a baked potato
Here to stay each day

First tea in the morning brew-er
List ticker, bidding do-er
Be we rich or be we poor
Here to stay each day

I will run your perfect bath
Wash the pots, cut the grass
Occasionally – make you laugh
Here to stay each day

It may be 24/7
Doesn't always feel like heaven
But that's just the way we're living
Here to stay each day

Isolated – but together
It won't always be forever
Here we are – come whatever
Here to stay each day

"A daily lifeline to sanity." *Frances Stanfield*

These Could Be The Good Old Days
#48 / 08:05:2020

These are the days
We will remember forever
If we are the lucky ones

Just like elderly relatives
Always mentioned the war
Our children will always remember "lockdown"

They will laugh about toilet rolls
Hand sanitiser, the importance of pasta
And how much DIY, gardening and exercise they did

They may even say the phrase
"Ah – the good old days
… when we actually had a National Health Service"

They may remember these
As times when strangers reached out
And we saw the best in people

They may even remember this
As when times changed – for the better
And we started to value each other
Key workers became the ordinary heroes
Politicians became accountable
And life became more important than mere economics

These might one day
Turn out to be "The Good Old Days"
If we can but learn

V.E. Day Celebrations
#49 / 09:05:2020

In these times, is this a day for celebration?
Is it ever a time for celebration?
How can we celebrate a victory
In the face of so much loss?

For, if we celebrate, then we glory
In the deaths of the "so called enemy"
Not the henchmen of Hitler
The co-conspirators of evil

But the everyday soldiers, airmen and sailors
Placed squarely in the firing line
The young forced into a uniform
Purely on the circumstances of birth, time and geography

Once you pass down the ranks
Privates, civilians ... there is no difference
We are all the same
We are all losers

And yet, we cannot help but be moved
By bravery, sacrifice and all the prices paid
As they made their mark in our history
And changed our lives

And for that, yes, we must remember, always
We must salute them and be proud
Proud of their dignity
Proud of the peace they won

Not celebration
But true commemoration

Another Day, Another Headline, Another Poem
#50 / 10:05:2020

Another day, another headline
Another day, another poem
Let's keep going
This plan is working
Mixed metaphors muddy and confuse
Road maps and menu options

But the question remains
What "plan" is that?
What planet are you on
If you think this is actually working?
More clichés
More empty rhetoric

We have to keep going
We have no choice
Same old words
Much like this poem

Haiku For Little Richard
#51 / 10:05:2020

If Noddy Holder
Says he wants to be like you
Then you are the king

A Mess Of Contradictions
#52 / 11:05:2020

Tally ho! It's back to work
Stay safe and stay alert
Understood?
Clear as mud

Stay Alert Boris
#53 / 11:05:2020

If we are to stay alert then it surely can't be wrong
To assume that you have been alert – right from day one
The facts would beg to differ, the dates don't really work
Too much un-noticed and not done if you had been alert

Twenty fourth and twenty ninth of Jan and Feb the fifth
Another on the twelfth – Cobra meetings missed
February the thirteenth – nothing at all
For a European Leaders' Conference Call

February fourteenth – Valentine
Holiday time so everything's fine
Eighteenth – another Cobra missed
Like COVID-19 just doesn't exist

And so it goes on and goes on and goes on
Emails are "lost" and chances are gone
You could follow the lead of leaders elsewhere
Take the advice from the knowledge they share

Learn from mistakes that others are making
You're too busy sleeping to think about waking
I'm no politician – no "so called" expert
But ...you cannot stay alert if you've never been alert

Alert to the dangers, alert to the facts
Alert to the truth, alert to act
Staying Alert, Staying Alert –
are the words you'd have us sing
But it's *Staying Alive* that we need –
your words don't mean a thing

Over To You
#54 / 12:05:2020

Stay Home and Save Lives – this message was clear
But because it's not working we're living in fear
That you might find out we could have done more
Than watching that horse bolt from our door

The plans have all changed – the trap has been set
The goal posts are moved – our cleverest yet
We've done what we can – we've done what we ought
So we're throwing the ball back into your court

You want us to move – you want us to act
We know you need work – exploiting that fact
We know you want "normal" – you're sick of the wait
So it's over to you to take up the bait

We've got a new slogan – to guide and advise
Carefully worded so we're not telling lies
A catchphrase, a jingle, a tagline so twee
A phrase that's so vague – you can't disagree

This piffle and waffle of meaningless phrases
Road maps and menus and nebulous phases
All this rhetoric, all this pretence
Of old fashioned British good common sense

If you're not careful – if you don't stay alert
If you contract the virus when you have to work
Then that is your choice – to do what you do
It's not down to us – so it's now up to you

Schools Can't Cope With An Outbreak Of Nits
But COVID-19 ... Dead Easy
#55 / 13:05:2020

Wash the pencils, gel the pens
Wipe the whiteboards twice and then
Bleach the toilets, mop the floors
Disinfect the corridors
Scrub the benches, clean the chairs
And bannisters on all the stairs
Ensure tables are pristine
Sanitise the plasticine
Cleanse the cutlery each day
Every plastic dinner tray
Every handle, every door
Do it once and then twice more
Move each desk before you start
Keep the pupils well apart
Wet-wipe books on all the shelves
Make the kids play by themselves
Wash the pencils, gel the pens
Then it's time to start again
Do this and more and I am guessing
You won't have time to teach a lesson

"Says it like it is." *Moira Andrew*

You Cannot Social Distance In A School
#56 / 14:05:2020

If adults cannot understand the concept and the fear
How can we expect the under-tens to hear
And act upon the nuances of this bad idea?
It may be in existence but you can't enforce the rule
You cannot social distance in a school

The nature of the classroom and the strength of education
Is unity, community and co-operation
How can that be possible in this situation?
It may be in existence but you can't enforce the rule
You cannot social distance in a school

Let's take the youngest children, remove them from their home
Where they've been safe and sound and make them sit alone
Where they can see the other lonely children on their own
It may be in existence but you can't enforce the rule
You cannot social distance in a school

You cannot tell a child that they cannot play with friends
Or that they have to work alone until the lesson ends
Is this the message that you really want to send?
It may be in existence but you can't enforce the rule
You cannot social distance in a school

We hear the old cliché ... "good old common sense"
But where's the common sense in this ill-thought-out pretence?
It's stupid and it's dangerous and there is no defence
It may be in existence but you can't enforce the rule
You cannot social distance in a school

It's "economics first" – or stubborn as a mule
For only the resistance and persistence of a fool
Would suggest this ignorance and policy so cruel
You cannot social distance
It is non-existent
You cannot social distance in a school

Let Our Teachers Be Heroes
#57 / 15:05:2020

The headlines scream in black and white
It's in the papers – it must be right
They're frontline workers – so fight the fight
Our teachers have always been heroes

This battle language, war of words
Means we're shaken and we're stirred
But hides the truth that can't be heard
Our teachers have always been heroes

They say the reasons staff don't act is
Militancy but the fact is
Safety first and good practice
Our teachers have always been heroes

Health and safety, risk assessment
That should be the first investment
Doesn't matter what the press meant
Our teachers have always been heroes

When the all-clear time arrives
That's the time for schools to thrive
Until then let's stay alive
Our teachers have always been heroes

All these clichés that you shout
Ill-prepared and ill-thought out
The poison and the lies you spout
Our teachers have always been heroes

Education – Education – Differentiation
#58 / 16:05:2020

Public schools – in September
State schools open in June
If it's not the same for everyone
Then right now is too soon

Public schools – well, not quite yet
State schools – yes, now is the time
That tells us what we want to know
Where priorities lie

Public schools – keep the gates closed
State – throw open the doors
One rule for the rich ...

Mr Hancock's Half Hour
#59 / 16:05:2020

You want "complete transparency"
In everything you say and do
You've got it, Mr Hancock
We can all see right through you

Blackbird On A Sunday Morning
#60 / 17:05:2020

The blackbird sings on fresh cut grass
With notes the angels understand
Heaven's song and evensong – a mass
An ode to this green pleasant land

A simple bird, the blackbird sings
And lightens every heart and every soul
Pure and shrill – he is the king
This song of songs, this purest gold

We're All In This Together
#61 / 17:05:2020

So, fill the House of Commons
Cram every seat and bench
Every nook and cranny
Let ministers of all persuasions
Stand shoulder to shoulder
Let our elected representatives
Represent us as they stare closely into each other's eyes
Let the chambers echo with words
Let speeches be punctuated with jeers
And coughs, cheers, high-fives, even the odd snore
Let there be standing room only
Let every member be present
Breathing the same hot air
Together

And when all this is done
Then and only then
Will we heed your words of bravery
And follow your leadership and example
Then will we congregate in classrooms
Fill our factory floors
Overflow the offices
Cheer on our football teams
And get back to normal

When you all go back to work
Then so shall we
Especially as we are all in this together
Good old-fashioned common sense isn't it?

"With Paul you are in safe and well washed hands." *Henry Normal*

Are You Sitting Comfortably?
Good, We Can Begin
#62 / 18:05:2020
Text for an unpublished and unpublishable picture book.

Hello boys and girls
This is Michael
Say hello to Michael

See Michael sitting alone
See his hair – all neatly brushed and combed
See Michael polish his spectacles
See Michael's lovely suit and straight tie
Smart Michael

See Michael try to smile
See how difficult it is for Michael
See his lips try to move
But Michael looks like a reptile
Poor Michael

Michael loves to read
Some of his best friends are books
See him turn the pages
Read – read – read – read – read
Clever Michael

Michael thinks he likes science too
He talks to people who are cleverer than him
But Michael doesn't listen
Because Michael thinks he is cleverer than them
See Michael cover his ears
Silly Michael

But Michael is strong
Very strong
Michael thinks he knows best
Even when his clever friends don't agree
So Michael carries on
Brave Michael

Michael knows lots of words
He likes to use them and show off
Michael likes the sound of his own voice
So Michael carries on talking
All the time
Loud Michael

Michael says things that aren't true
Michael knows they aren't true
But still he says them
Because Michael thinks he knows best
Naughty Michael

Look boys and girls
You can tell when Michael is telling fibs
See Michael's mouth moving
Every time it moves, he tells naughty fibs and lies
Bad Michael

But Michael doesn't mind
Michael doesn't care
Michael doesn't care at all
Very bad Michael

Do you believe in monsters, boy and girls?
Not all monsters have sharp horns
Big teeth and nasty claws
Some have neat hair, spectacles
And lovely neat ties
Monstrous Michael

"Lovely ridicule." *Andy Camp*

He Was
#63 / 19:05:2020

He was an amazing man
One of the best
One of my favourite people

He was wonderful and caring
One of the loveliest
We were lucky to have known him

He was lovely
Truly a gentleman
And a true gentleman

He was delightful and amazing
A hero in every way
Always a good friend

He was special
A massive heart
One of the nicest men I've ever met

Scrolling down comments
Reading cards
Our eyes fill up

Not just because of the truth
But because of the word
"Was"

Aftermath
#64 / 20:05:2020

The birds sang
The sun shone
In the midst of life there is death

Social distancing – maybe
But together we gathered
Together we mourned

A fireman's guard of honour
A fitting tribute, respect and integrity
We all saluted you

Heartfelt words and memories resonate
Much loved music fills the air
As we remembered ... remembered

Love divine – all loves excelling
The Lord is my shepherd
The comfort of faith and prayer

Wood, brass and dust
Flowers, soil and marble
Tears, love and goodbyes

All the clichés present
But clichés are the truth
Worlds turned upside down

The birds shone
The sun sang
In the midst of death there was life

You

Missed
#65 / 21:05:2020

I hit the post, the ball bounced out
Let's call it a goal anyway
Number nineteen in the top forty
Call it number one, well waddayasay?

I owe you a pound, here's eighty pee
Let's say you're paid in full
I drew my bow, the arrow flew
Grazed the white – let's call it bull

You promised us a target
But your numbers don't add up
You promised us a target
And now it's "ifs" and "buts"

A hundred-thousand tests a day
By the time we reach the first of May
Not there by a long chalk
But hey, it's okay

Because you tried, you really tried
You said you've done your level best
Because you're there or thereabouts
Let's say you've passed the test

Just like those who had exams
A-levels, GCSE
Now they can have an A
When once predicted C

Nowhere near your SATs?
Never mind – you've passed
Under these new rules
No-one need come last

Richard Coles, Anne Widdecombe
Strictly King and Queen
Eddie the Eagle – gold
Champions League for every team

To be pragmatic with mathematics
It's either wrong or right
Numbers do not lie
It's there in black and white

You invented this number
No spin – and no twist
You set your very own targets
… And still you missed

Too
#66 / 22:05:2020

Too little	Too flippant
Too late	To care
Too trite	Too stupid
Too vague	To think
Too muddled	Too long
Too often	To wait
Too mixed	Too short
Too casual	Term view
Too few	Too great
Too sensible	A risk
Too numerous	Too much
Too selfish	To lose

Too many
Will die

Too true

Comings And Goings
#67 / 23:05:2020

So … surprise, surprise
One rule for you
And a different one for us

You gave advice to the nation
You set guidelines for the general public

For others

The arrogance of power
The ignorance of responsibility

How can we trust you now?
If we ever did

Others have resigned for similar acts
Of defiance and stupidity

No doubt you won't

But we all know you should
Like you knew you shouldn't travel

Two hundred and fifty miles
But you did

Cummings and going
Let's hope so

Not So Very Long Ago
#68 / 24:05:2020

Not so very long ago
A politician was derided, demeaned and demonised
For wearing a coat deemed shabby
And a tie not properly knotted

Now we have a Prime Minister
Incapable of brushing his own hair in a tidy manner
And an adviser in a hoody, beanie hat, untucked shirt
And coat that could be deemed shabby

No derision, demeaning, demonisation

Recently, another politician was accused of
Having a field
To ridicule, spin and slander

Today we have
Someone who made the rules
Then broke the rules – deliberately

There are lies, untruths, cover-ups
Inconsistencies – to say the very least – abound
The hypocrisy of all being in this together

No derision, demeaning or demonisation

"Maverick ally" says The Daily Mail
And for once they are
Almost right

Maverick
A liar

Meanwhile, In Other News ...
Arctic Penguin Poop Gives Off Laughing Gas
#69 / 25:05:2020

You can stay at home or stay alert
These messages – irrational
Just what is social distancing?
Confusion that is national
The death toll rises higher
From what has come to pass
Meanwhile – in other news
Arctic penguin poop gives off laughing gas

Well, Dominic's "responsible"
And "acted legally"
The "instincts of a father"
With "integrity"
So says Boris Johnson
In a briefing brash and crass
Meanwhile – in other news
Arctic penguin poop gives off laughing gas

Spin the lies and twist the truth
Is that all you do?
You want complete transparency
We see through all of you
Undermining sacrifices
Playing loose and fast
Meanwhile – in other news
Arctic penguin poop gives off laughing gas

Disregard for guidelines
They sought to implement
One rule for the rulers
Is what they really meant
Double-standards, double-talk
Lies and lies en masse
Meanwhile – in other news
Arctic penguin poop gives off laughing gas

Even your supporters scream
"What planet are you on?"
You must have failed when The Mail
Thinks you have done wrong
You cannot do the right thing
You can't show any class
Meanwhile – in other news
Arctic penguin poop gives off laughing gas

A penguin's defecation
Leads to gaseous emissions
Like the proclamations of
A minister's decisions
But it's no laughing matter
When the opposite is true
When Boris Johnson talks
We all can smell the poo

We might see your mouth move
But you're talking through your ass
Meanwhile – in other news
Arctic penguin poop gives off laughing gas

A straw that breaks the camel's back
Well, maybe this is it
When Boris Johnson talks
We all can smell the shit

This Poem Is True
#70 / 26:05:2020

This poem is true
It contains words that all exist in the dictionary

These words are not fake or false
So, this poem is true

All the words in this poem are real
No words have been invented

They are words we all know
So, this poem is true

No words have been mispronounced
All are spelt correctly

They are all every day, reasonable words
So, this poem is true

Words like "family", "childcare" and "sickness"
Words we can easily agree with
Words we can all relate to

Words like "worried" and "wife"
"Car" and "castle"
Good examples of alliteration

This poem uses real words
But does not tell the full story

Because this poem is sometimes forgetful
Some words have been left out

But, nevertheless, this poem is true
In that all the words here are real words
This poem chooses its words very carefully

It does not use words we have all been using
Like "responsibility", "all in this together"
Or "stay at home"

This poem will not apologise
For this glaring omission
And why should it?

You have read all the words
And these words are real
So, this poem is true

This poem knows the difference
Between honesty and truth
So, this poem is being very careful

No Regrets
#71 / 27:05:2020

This story will not go just yet
But there are no regrets
Oblivious to those upset
But there are no regrets

It may be tricky and complex
But guidelines are the ones you set
Not the spirit we expect
Or the standards we accept
But there are no regrets

An own goal in the home team net
Like a jelly not quite set
Or shifting sand that's soaking wet
An example that you didn't set
But there are no regrets

The strangest facts that you select
The dots are there but don't connect
It doesn't even feel correct
Lost the plots and lost respect
But there are no regrets
Just what is it that you don't get?

No regrets that we thought twice
Followed government advice
Made a personal sacrifice
Isolated – paid the price

No regrets you undermined
A national mood that tried to find
A way through this that's helpful, kind
Ignorant? Or are you blind?

What do you not understand?
What makes you so underhand?
You give us cause to wonder and
Question why you're in demand

When your fiction's unbelievable
Logic inconceivable
But you think it's achievable
That your position is retrievable

Arrogant and bulletproof
Condescending and aloof
Would it hurt to tell the truth?
Prove you've not a cloven hoof

And still you've no regrets?
Still you've no regrets?
Elite and heartless hypocrites
Move on – no regrets

"I love the way you speak for all of us – but so much better
than we could." *Shirley Smith*

I Think That I'm In Love With Emily Maitlis
#72 / 28:05:2020

We all live in troubled times, days unprecedented
Isolating, hibernating, going quite demented
But if there is a lining that is silver then it's this
I think that I'm in love with Emily Maitlis

The downside is the doom and gloom, the stories in the press
Political shenanigans, an ever-growing mess
But if there is an upside, then the upside is
I'm seeing so much more of Emily Maitlis

A woman of intelligence and blessed with common sense
Like a knife through butter re the government's intents
Dominic's short comings, the spin, the lies, the twist
That's why I think we are in love with Emily Maitlis

She says just what we're thinking and says it honestly
Yet reprimanded and removed by the BBC
Views right here on Newsnight – so how can they dismiss
The queen who's been upon our screen – Emily Maitlis

Emily's no enemy – the voice of truth for you and me
Emily – the remedy – is plain and clear for all to see
Newsnight doesn't feel quite right – the presence that we miss
That's why we all love you – Emily Maitlis

Civic Duty
#73 / 29:05:2020

I'll gladly do my civic duty
And not visit castles of natural beauty

In The Interests Of Impartiality
#74 / 29:05:2020

This
Poem
Will
Take
A
Neutral
Stance
And
Show
No
Political
Bias
Left
Or
Right
It
Will
Not
Name
Any
Public
Figures
Deemed
To
Have
Questions
Hanging
Over
Their
Suitability
For
Public
Service
This
Poem
Is
Perfect
For
Newsnight

A Happy Song For Us To Sing To Celebrate The Fact
We Are No. 1 In Europe ... In The Death Toll Charts
#75 / 30:05:2020

The sun has got his hat on
Hip – hip – hip – hooray
We're not down in lockdown
And everything's okay

Things are back to normal
And COVID's gone away
Cos ... the sun has got his hat on
And six of us can play

Dominic and Boris
Both have had their say
Even though they both should go
Both of them will stay

The sun has got his hat on
Hip – hip – hip – hooray
Yes, the sun has got his hat on
And we're coming out to play

Fifteen in a classroom
It's the perfect way
For moving on and staying safe
Let us not delay

The sun has got his hat on
Hip – hip – hip – hooray
The sun has got his hat on
And it's barbecues today

Down By The Riverbank
#76 / 31:05:2020

It was good to get out
More than good, great

A walk down by the riverbank
Sunshine, shorts, shades

The serenade of birdsong
And the perfect breeze

A few families sat in groups
Children splashed and laughed

A dog couldn't resist the lure of water
Neither could two teenagers

Who jumped fearlessly
Then couldn't get out quick enough

A comical crow picked and pecked
At a crisp packet on the riverbank

And I remembered childhood days
Bike rides and blue skies

The fascination of water
However cold, green and slimy

And family picnics on riverbanks
Meat paste sandwiches, diluted squash and budget crisps

And when it was time to go mum and dad
Would make sure we packed up all our litter

And any other bits of rubbish
Before we went home

Down by the riverbank
With the sunshine, the breeze, the birdsong

And crisp packets and cans

Prayer For The First Day Of School
#77 / 01:06:2020

God bless the teachers in this new test
God bless the children as they try their best
God bless the parents – now worried alone
God bless all those who kept theirs at home

Give them all wisdom, kindness and strength
Patience and thoughtfulness, good common sense
May there be laughter, may there be fun
As they work together to get this thing done

But most of all Lord
In this new unknown
Keep them all safe
And bring them all home

When The First Child Dies In School
#78 / 01:06:2020

When the first child dies in school
Then will you say that this was the right time?

When someone's son or daughter is lost
Because of an infection passed on in the playground
Will you still stand by your call
For schools to have opened so soon?

Or will you blame the teachers for dereliction of duty
And not following procedures?

Health. Safety. Life.
More important than grades right now

Let the teachers get it right
As they always have

The Truth That's In The Bible Is Lost Because Of You
#79 / 02:06:2020

You give God a bad name every time you talk about him
You make it so easy – to think of life without him
You are the perfect reason – for everyone to doubt him
I cannot see Jesus in anything you do
The truth that's in The Bible is lost because of you

You glory in the story of riches stored in heaven
Redemption and salvation and sins that are forgiven
But then ignore so many more and the poverty they live in
You say you care and offer prayer – but that is nothing new
The truth that's in The Bible is lost because of you

You talk of love thy neighbour when your heart is full of hate
No time to feed the hungry when you've so much on your plate
You say good things will come – to those who pray and wait
Condescending, patronising, blinkered point of view
The truth that's in The Bible is lost because of you

Hypocrisy your middle name – you spell it differently
You think it's P-R-I-N-C-I-P and L and E
The sermon on the mount is a page you didn't see
Salvation is for everyone and not the chosen few
The truth that's in The Bible is lost because of you

Your narrow-minded views mean that your heart's forever closed
Compassion is a foreign word for those less indisposed
Empathy and sympathy – both undiagnosed
If faith has a sticking point – you must be the glue
The truth that's in The Bible is lost because of you

You talk of being godly – when plainly you are not
Instead pride and prejudice are qualities you've got
Judge that ye be not judged – something you forgot
The fact that you are lying is the only thing that's true
The truth that's in The Bible is lost because of you

You say that you believe but you don't understand
That faith and compassion go hand in hand in hand
Your excuse for doing nothing is that God had got it planned

You think you know what's right but you haven't got a clue
The truth that's in The Bible is lost because of you

You think that being holy is silence and respect
But silence is a wholly inappropriate concept
Sometimes you've got to shout against the violence and neglect
Change is like your library books – too long overdue
The truth that's in The Bible is lost because of you

You read that Jesus washes sins away whiter than white
But whiter than white is not a phrase we need tonight
Hiding from the truth in a White House with no light
Darkness and division and tear gas on cue
The truth that's in The Bible is lost because of you

Take The Knee
#80 / 03:06:2020

Solidarity
Take the knee
Equality
Take the knee
Democracy
Take the knee
Unity
Take the knee
Community
Take the knee
Empathy
Take the knee
Humility
Take the knee
Apology
Take the knee
You, me
Take the knee
Everybody
Take the knee

The President And The Bible
#81 / 04:06:2020

Blasphemous, irreverent
The photo of the President

The Bible is not resident
In the White House of the President

Jesus is not evident
In the actions of the President

Godliness – irrelevant
In the outlook of the President

Ignorance that's eloquent
In the backlash of the President

Only stone and sediment
In the hard heart of the President

No room needs this elephant
The presence of this President

Darkness that's malevolent
Prevalent in this President

"A daily poem that made it worth getting up for."
Chris Radford

Hell Raiser

#82 / 05:06:2020
for Steve Priest

Top of the Pops
Was always worth watching because of you
If only to see what our dads would say

We hadn't got a clue – what to do!
But we still said it like you
In the schoolyard on a Friday

Dodgy make up
Hot pants and Red Indian head-dresses
German helmets and silver platform boots

And always a knowing smile
A wink to the camera
A pout, a kiss and a flounce

We didn't know what "camp" was then
We just knew it was fun
Especially with you

Not moody, mysterious or mystical
But underrated because you smiled
You rocked and rolled and entertained

And that's why we remember
That's why we loved you
We were ready Steve

Too Much To Ask?
#83 / 05:06:2020

The death toll ever rising
You failing in your task
Isn't it a little late
To suggest that we all wear a mask?

Surely the time for action
Was way back in the past?
So why now? Why and how?
Should we now wear a mask?

You gambled with our lives
The die – it has been cast
And now and only now you say
That we all should wear a mask?

You didn't close the airports
The lockdown didn't last
Suddenly – it's common sense
That everyone should wear a mask?

Guidelines that aren't followed
Back to normal far too fast
A practical solution
Ooh – let's all wear a mask

Is the question difficult?
Is it too much to ask
Why? Oh why? Oh why? Oh why
Is now the time to wear a mask?

Phone Call From A Friend
#84 / 06:06:2020

Finally, we talked
Missed calls, months passed
A few texts here and there
But finally we talked … and talked

Of families and illness
The state of the world
How our lives have changed
And the ways we now fill our time

Not gigs on the road and tours
But ways to roast a chicken
Or baste a pork joint
Spice racks and whether we've ever used cumin

We were never rock and roll
But we miss the audience connection
The interaction of voices
And the communion of something special

Remembering Steve Priest and the like
Childhood days revisited
Waiting for our dad's predictability
With those glam rock ugly sisters

Time passed easily, time passed quickly
Eulogising over the genius of 'How Does it Feel'
'Tiger Feet' and how bands that had a laugh
Were never given the credit they deserved

Mutual musical recommendations
Common ground excavated
It was great not to be isolated
To make contact, to laugh, really laugh

We said that maybe we'd write a song
My words – your music and voice
But if we don't, no worries
It was just great to hear your voice

Next time we'll talk for even longer
Face to face
With good quality beer
Cheers John, cheers

Malady In The UK
#85 / 07:06:2020

In the first days of lockdown
When streets were empty
Town centres ghostly
Strangely, there was hope

People helped each other
Took it all seriously
Clapped the NHS from doorsteps
Isolation meant isolation

It felt like there was hope
A chance to change
A time to somehow start again
Something new

All gone now
Worse than it's ever been
Clamouring for normality
In the face of mortality

Social distancing ignored
Gathering to drink and litter
Or protest, march – and worse
Mixed messages and chaos

Government – a laughing stock
Clowns – but no jokes
Deadly serious pantomime
But this is not behind us

Oh no it isn't

Weekend Haiku Thoughts
#86 / 08:06:2020

If statues must fall
From when black lives were worthless
Tear these relics down

Black lives must matter
And white lives must understand
Now more than ever

No grey areas
What is right is right is right
These lives must matter

Are We Being Served?
#87 / 09:06:2020

Like an out-of-date sitcom
All catchphrases and stereotypes
Predictable plots and quotable lines
But are we being served?

The joke seems to be on us
As the Prime Minister makes a cameo
Like young Mister Grace as the credits roll
Saying "You're all doing very well!"

Meanwhile …
We have all been watching

Empathy Day Or ... Irony Day?
#88 / 10:06:2020

On Empathy Day
You spoke of tolerance and
How black lives matter

The same empathy
When talking "picaninnies"
"Watermelon smiles"?

**Lesson – The Danger ...
Or Is It Lessen The Danger?**
#89 / 10:06:2020

Stop – start – school – all of this mess meant
Ineffective risk assessment
Differing views – changing lately
Inconclusive health and safety

I'm Forever Bursting ...
#90 / 11:06:2020

We've got a new term
To help us all learn
But the problem and the trouble is
We don't have a clue
Just what we should do
We don't know what a bubble is

Sometimes
#91 / 12:06:2020

Sometimes it's affirmation
Sometimes collaboration
Sometimes we need creation
Just to get through

Sometimes it's family
A friend reaching out to me
Sometimes it's poetry
Just to get through

Sometimes it's resistance
To anti-social distance
Asking for your assistance
Just to get through

Lose myself with Stephen King
Listening to Michael sing
Sometimes the little things
Just to get through

Sometimes it's not enough
To be loved by the ones you love
Sometimes it's other stuff
Just to get through

Sometimes you've got to say
Today's a day that's not okay
Tomorrow is another day
Just to get through

The Singer Sings His Song – With A Poet's Heart
#92 / 13:06:2020
for Michael McDermott

Every word is sacred
Not a word is wasted
Heavy with their truth, they hit every single mark

Every word is vital
Every line and every title
The singer sings his song – with a poet's heart

Every word is real
Nothing is concealed
Honesty that's harrowing, each heart string torn apart

Every word is open
Every word is broken
The singer sings his song – with a poet's heart

Every word has meaning
A reason for believing
Precious like the diamonds, shining in the dark

Depth and understanding
Important and demanding
The singer sings his song – with a poet's heart

Every word is whole
Directly from the soul
Reaching out to touch us – with a healing spark

Every word connects us
A hit to the solar plexus
The singer sings his song – with a poet's heart

The power of the story
The pain and then, the glory
The singer sings his song – with a poet's heart

Every word is honest
Reflecting what's upon us
The poet writes his poems with a singer's art

Welcome Back
#93 / 13:06:2020

COVID times, Twitter frozen
We miss all the words you've chosen
Poet, friend – to those who knows him
Michael – risen, Michael Rosen

Truth
#94 / 14:06:2020

Trouble in these troubled times
Join the dots and see the signs
Try to read between the lines
Looking for the truth

Liberty for statues
Monuments as public loos
Can't believe what's in the news
Just what is the truth

Protest and resistance
Singing songs of Winston's
Shouting their insistence
Standing up for truth

Saluting like a Nazi
Polluting all our history
Diluting all the bravery
Pissing on the truth

Honouring all those deceased
All the ones who died for peace
By picking fights with police
Fighting for the truth

Black lives, white lives
Fake news and Twitter lies
Those who cry the loudest cries
Shouting for the truth

Just who is fighting who
Nobody has got a clue
What is false and what is true
Questioning the truth

Trouble in these troubled times
Join the dots and see the signs
Try to read between the lines
Looking for the truth

Saint Patrick's Day
#95 / 15:06:2020

Patrick Hutchinson

Did the right thing
Amidst the throng of wrong

An act of selflessness
When the moment was heated

An act of calmness
When all around was chaos

An act of peace
In the theatre of hate

An act of bravery
In the time of need

He wasn't heavy
He wasn't your brother

But you carried him to safety
Leant him on your shoulder

A living example
Compassion and equality

The Twelfth of June
A new Saint Patrick's Day

I'm Not Looking Forward To Football Again
#96 / 16:06:2020

I'm not looking forward to football again
Not missing the beautiful game
My team are unbeaten since I don't know when
I'm glad to be free of the strain

I'm not looking forward to football again
It's starting but won't be the same
No doubt about it, since I've been without it
I've not had the heartache and pain

My nerves are un-shredded, my pulse rate is even
Moods – they don't dip or change
No agitation, no aggravation
My passion, it seems on the wane

I'm not really bothered but no hesitation
Now football is starting again
I've not missed the depression
But here's my confession
I'll probably watch every game

In A League Of His Own
#97 / 17:06:2020

No matter our team, no matter our allegiance, we support Marcus
All children matter – nobody should go hungry – thank you to Marcus

If we do not care for those who have the least then we don't care at all
It's all kicking off, number ten to number ten – PM met his match

Prime mover, great finish, already you have scored the goal of the season
One Marcus Rashford, only one Marcus Rashford – we all sing your name

Problem Or Solution
#98 / 18:06:2020

Protest or anarchy
Clarity or sanity
Trying to hold on to what is our humanity

Fighting inequality
Rewriting history
Statues falling in the name of liberty

Chaos and confusion
Truth is an illusion
Bigotry and hatred, power and delusion

Black lives, white lies
Don't know who to patronise
No matter how it is described it is still apartheid

No disputing
Rioting and looting
Nobody's a winner when there's tear gas and shooting

Revolution starter
Ripping up the charter
Who you going to deify and who you going to martyr

Don't know what's next
Got to find context
As long as it's not some cop's knees on a neck

Fact or fiction
Duty dereliction
Fake news, twitter views, run for re-election
It's all getting tribal
There won't be revival
With a phony president posing with a Bible

Great Britain, USA
History won't go away
No matter what you say, things are not okay KK

Apologies your majesty
Your birthday was a tragedy
Loyalty to royalty transforming into travesty

Aiming for Churchillian
Vile and vaudevillian
Swastikas and Sieg Heils, repulsive and reptilian

Twitter chatter
All lives matter
True that they do but try it when they're blacker

Everybody says this
I am not a racist
Heads full of ignorance and far too scared to face this

Don't be selective
Got to get perspective
Tolerate intolerance – always ineffective

Be analytical
When everything's political
Be what you want to be but don't be hypocritical

You say you're not the problem
But this is the conclusion

You're part of the problem
At the heart of the problem
If you don't start the redemption and solution

Always the problem
Always the problem
Always the problem
Never the solution

Songbird
#99 / 19:06:2020
for Dame Vera Lynn

Your voice, synonymous with war
Your songs of love and peace
Like the girl who sang next door
Of hope and sweet release

Of sweethearts who will re-unite
Whenever that may be
Bluebirds flying, cliffs of white
If we just wait and see

The purest melody that starts
For every woman, every man
An angel voice that caught our hearts
Like everybody's favourite nan

Timeless songs live ever more
Thanks to you, Dame Vera
Fare thee well, we sing along
The ending of an era

Tired
#100 / 20:06:2020

I'm tired of writing angry poems
Tired of being frustrated
Tired of depressing headlines
To be honest, I'm just tired

Tired of watching the news
Tired of shouting at the television
Tired of the excuses and lies
Really tired

Tired of endless days the same
Tired of wearing these clothes again
Tired of isolation and silence
Just tired

Tired of not being able to work
Tired of the uncertainty
I'm not doing a great deal
But I'm still tired

If this is tired
Don't want to be retired

"Thanks for doing this Paul - we need it." *Catherine Obbard*

All The World Is A Plague – A Sonnet
#101 / 20:06:2020

This lexicon of emptiness rings out
This condescending clanging of a bell
Cliched platitudes leave us in no doubt
Your hands-on handles on the cart to hell

Unprecedented times though these may be
These levels of ineptitude just rise
Everyone is shouting – at you on the TV
As questions go unanswered with the lies

This bumbling trickery with smiling face
The frippery of painting of a plane
A shameful farce the waste of track and trace
A footballer who doesn't have a name

Shakespearean is something he would be
A comedy of errors – that is he

Boris – On It? Boris – Sonnet
#102 / 21:06:2020

Well – erm – ha – harrumph – er – well – ha – you see
Sentences – er – gaps – and – I'm – er … perplexed
Ahem – ah – waffle – piffle aimlessly
No idee-ah – which words – um – come out … … next

Absolutely! Hmmm – and – cough – and-and-and
Aha – you see – I – I – I – I – mutter
A random pause – erm – I – don't – und – errr – stand
If in doubt – st – st – st – st – stutter

Yes – yes – yes – yes – I mean it – standing here
Proud and in control – total and complete
Let me be transparent and quite clear
Repeat – repeat – repeat – repeat … repeat

Feigned sincerity – this art of bluffing
Much ado – as usual – about nothing

Today's News – In Limerick Form
#103 / 22:06:2020

While life is generally rubbish
What needs to be understood is
In trivial news
The blues didn't lose
And these poems are going to be published

Ignorance Is Bliss
#104 / 23:06:2020

White lives matter says the banner on the plane
Golliwogs on Facebook – but it's just fun and games
I've got a black friend and I treat them just the same
As the saying goes, ignorance is bliss
No. Ignorance is this

You say you like reggae, hip hop and rap
And you applaud all the sports stars who are black
But still you want Great Britain back
As the saying goes, ignorance is bliss
No. Ignorance is this

It isn't being snowflake, it isn't being woke
It isn't just a laugh and it isn't just a joke
White lives matter – sorry that I spoke
As the saying goes, ignorance is bliss
No. Ignorance is this

Open up your eyes, everything's subliminal
Do what you can – even if it's minimal
You say that you won't take the knee for a criminal
As the saying goes, ignorance is bliss
No. Ignorance is this

Don't get diverted, distracted or annoyed
By what you think you know about George Floyd
Jumping to conclusions is something to avoid
As the saying goes, ignorance is bliss
No. Ignorance is this

Look at the cause and not the catalyst
Look at the reasons why this movement must exist
Otherwise, every single point is missed
As the saying goes, ignorance is bliss
No. Ignorance is this

The twistery of history, the right and the wrong
More than just a statue and more than just a song
Ask every question if we are to move along

As the saying goes, ignorance is bliss
No. Ignorance is this

Equality's a quality that's only ever real
Where everybody starts on a level playing field
That didn't happen, that's why everyone should kneel
As the saying goes, ignorance is bliss
Don't let ignorance be this

No More Daily Briefings
#105 / 24:06:2020

No more Daily Briefings
No more looking for Boris
Just in case he appears
Where he mumbles and errs
Before passing over to the suits either side
The taking a long time
To tell us absolutely nothing
Apart from contradictory platitudes

No more Daily Briefings
No more daily wastes of time
No more games of "Who is that?"
Where ministers we've never heard of
Stand behind sloganned podiums
Armed with only clichés and half-truths
As they try and tell us that
The UK is doing very well
Indeed

Not the best TV on screen
Not one of those "must-see-things"
Nothing that we're going to miss
No more Daily Briefings

Back To Life – Back To Reality?
#106 / 25:06:2020

Back to the pubs, the salons, the shops
As long as you stay a metre away
Have they really chosen the fourth of July
So it sounds like Independence Day?

Just what has happened to Track and Trace?
No vaccinations for those that are ill
Last time we looked at the figures
People were dying still … still

If lockdown is easing are we on the mend?
Has COVID-19 just gone away?
Or are we just bored, impatient and stupid
To think we are safe and we'll be okay?

Hindsight
#107 / 26:06:2020

Hindsight, blindsight
Wrap it up how you like
Waiting for the next wave
Waiting for the second spike

Doctors that are tireless
Nurses that inspire us
All these scientists
And still we've got the virus

Churchill Would Be Proud
#108 / 27:06:2020

Blame it on the sunshine
The weather and humidity
Unprecedented times
Equalled with stupidity
Lockdown breakout causes
Police and peace-less breaches
Churchill would be proud
There was fighting on the beaches

Drink and drugs and barbecues
It's a Bournemouth D-Day
Anti-social distancing
Where the beach becomes a bidet
Invasion of the stupid
The lemmings, louts and leeches
Churchill would be proud
There was fighting on the beaches

A sad, sad day for common sense
Mob culture and mob rules
A buzzing swarm of selfishness
The gathering of the fools
The second spike that we should fight
Now looms within our reaches
Churchill would be proud
There was fighting on the beaches

Freedom is a basic right
Well worth fighting for
We're all in this together
But this is not the war
So learn from recent history
The harsh truth that it teaches
This virus is alive and viral
It will multiply and spiral
The second wave could well be tidal
And we're fighting on the beaches?

He Wants His Churchill Moment
#109 / 28:06:2020

He wants his Churchill moment
You can tell it from his speeches
"We'll wrestle this mugger to the ground"
Fight it on the bleaches

He wants his Churchill moment
So when all this is over
It's spitfires, waffle and we'll meet
By white cliffs at Dover

He wants his Churchill moment
All fuss and bluff and bluster
And all the British bulldog
Spirit he can muster

He wants his Churchill moment
This leader who'll inspire us
Just because his legacy
Is he survived the virus

He wants his Churchill moment
Assurance and endurance
But he's more like the Churchill
That dog that sells insurance

He wants his Churchill moment
Tactician, soldier, hunter
But half of him is Flashman
Crossed with Billy Bunter

He wants his Churchill moment
A soundbite and smokescreen
We'll double down to level up
Whatever that may mean

Too little too late – too much too soon
Every *ummm* and every *aaah*
He wants his Churchill moment
Not even close – and no cigar

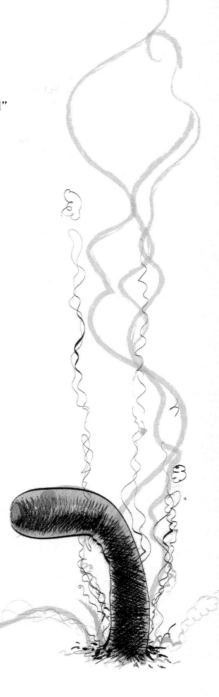

Fit As A Butcher's Dog
#110 / 29:06:2020

Press ups for the press
Even in my Sunday best
A shirt and tie and – yes
You've got to be impressed

Every day I exercise
Every day I jog
Bouncing back, on the attack
I'm fit as a butcher's dog

Fit as a butcher's dog you say
While smiling all agog
Fat on all the prime cuts
Now that's more like a butcher's dog

Detectives most perceptive
In this national time of need
Detectives are detecting
An increase in my speed

Back in Number Ten again
Like falling off a log
Full of beans, I'm lean and keen
Fit as a butcher's dog

Fit as a butcher's dog you say
Well – a bulldog's what you ain't
More Old English Sheepdog
Selling whitewash and gloss paint

At home I'm present and involved
In a detailed way
What all of those details are
I really cannot say

Happy to get stuck in though
Happy to do my slog
Oh yes, I changed a nappy once
Fit as a butcher's dog

Fit as a butcher's dog you say
Fit as a butcher's dog
A hound we've found that likes to sound off
Going the whole hog

Fit as a butcher's dog you say
Happy and eager to please
Like puppy that's excited
At its owner's knees

Fit as a butcher's dog you say
Getting treats for tricks
Lots of porky pies
Fetching back your master's sticks

Fit as a butcher's dog you say
Your pedigree chum keeps humming
Chop-chop – this butcher's shop
All its staff and all its stock
All the lot that you have got
Owned by a Mr Cummings

"Fabulous." *Kim Hopper*

So Many Reasons, Mister Rosen
#111 / 30:06:2020

Michael
You are back
We did not know about that fifty-fifty chance
But we are so glad that you woke up
And that the coma was a comma, not a full stop

Michael
So pleased you're back with us
Much more than just much loved
More than very much missed
A national living treasure

Michael
We know your words so well
Everybody's favourite uncle
With our favourite stories and jokes
The one who pulls the funny faces
Especially when you shouldn't

Michael
You may feel feeble and lopsided
Like your legs are cardboard tubes full of porridge
But you've gone from horizontal to hobbling

Sticky McStickstick
A stick for walking is better than not walking at all
Plus it's something to wave at the telly
When your beloved Arsenal frustrate you
As indeed they will

Michael
We look forward to hearing your voice again
Reading new poems
Re-reading old poems
Retweeting all those tweets

But Michael
Sorry – we must be patient, as you have been
Leave you alone to relax, recover, gain strength
And not be distracted by our well-wishes, however kind
Or poems like this

Michael
We are glad that you are back

Michael – the voice of reason
Michael – the voice of Rosen

Boz The Builder
#112 / 01:07:2020

Boz the builder – can he fix it?
Boz the builder – yes he can!

Hard hat – hi-viz – forklift driver
Photo-op – well fulfilled
He has a got a message for us
We are going to build – build – build

Three words that he can remember
One word, three times – he is thrilled
He repeats it – and repeats it
And repeats it – build – build – build

Boz the builder – can he fix it?
Boz the builder – thinks he can

We can battle any crisis
Many workers – highly skilled
Diggers, tractors – they'll distract us
When they start to build – build – build

Let's all clap the wealth creators
Bankers, merchants – of the guild
Working together to get the job done
You will all be billed – billed – billed

Boz the builder – can he fix it?
Project Speed – spend – spend – spend
Bodge the builder – here's to Brexit
We will all pay in the end

Let Me Tell You How I Count The Days
#113 / 02:07:2020

I count the days in custard creams
Today – seventeen

I mark the hours with cups of tea
A personal record – twenty-three

Every quarter of an hour I need
To see my latest twitter feed

Another twenty – such an age
Count the likes on my Facebook page

Wander round the house a bit
Pick a book up, look at it

Kettle on – another cup
Catch up on the washing up

Telly on – flick around
Sit down – get up – sit back down

Messenger and email checks
Solitaire – read a text

Click the mouse – surf the net
Who my team is playing next

Toilet time – magazine
Articles already seen

Notebook open – pick up pen
Three lines later – down again

YouTube lotto, Instagram
It may be vague – but it's a plan

Let me count up all the ways
To fill the time on lockdown days

Can't Wait For Saturday Night
#114 / 03:07:2020

I'd love to go down the pub again
Too long a wait for a night with friends

I've missed the crack, the atmosphere
Football chatter, hand-pulled beer

Things may start with good intentions
Two pints later – not a mention

No such thing as social distance
Another pint – no resistance

Have another mate – it'll be right
You won't catch COVID here tonight

Fuzzy haze – defences drop
No control – too late to stop

The blurred, the slurred, the slow to think
Potential danger with every drink

I'd love to go down to the pub again
But when it's safe – I'll go there then

Opening Time?
#115 / 03:07:2020

Anyone drinking in the pub'll
At 6 a.m. be asking for
trouble

Dear Prime Minister
#116 / 03:07:2020

I shan't call you "Boris"
As people may think that implies friendship
And I shan't refer to you as "Mister"
As that signifies respect

I think I'll leave out the "Dear" too

So, Prime Minister
You had a chance – a real once in a lifetime chance

You could have united the nation
With decisive leadership
Direct and immediate action
A brave and direct approach
But you just couldn't do it

You could have led the way
From a position of authority and majority
Built a legacy, something memorable
Left your opponents way behind

Imagine if you had reached out to the NHS and beyond
Publicly praised them all as the jewels in our crown
And backed it up with appropriate budgets and wages structures
In making them heroes
You would have yourself been the hero maker

You could have been honest
About your chief advisor's lies
Sacked him and gained a nation's respect
You could have brought people together
Done all this and more
This door was open for you
But you dithered
Ummed and *ahhed*
Blustered and ultimately said nothing of note

It took a young footballer
To teach you empathy, heart and compassion

Prime Minister
That could have been you
That should have been you
You could have been remembered as
The People's Prime Minister
Who showed us the way in difficult times
Led us in – dare we say it – unprecedented times
You even survived the virus
You could have been a national hero
You had your chance
Amidst this can of worms you had your chance
Yet you could not take it
You could not do it
Yes, Prime Minister
You blew it

I Will Not Take The Knee
#117 / 04:07:2020

I will not take the knee
So says our brave Prime Minister
Principled, strong words
Or something much more sinister?

I will not take the knee
I don't believe in gestures
Yet still I clap the NHS
Applaud all our investors

I will not take the knee
I believe in things substantial
Like capital and merchant banks
And everything financial

I must remain impartial
Unbiased and apart
No suggestion that a gesture
Is an action of my heart

But ...

Your life is one big cliché
Gestures – you've made plenty
Most of them embarrassing
Pitiful and empty

You want something of substance
Not dead down in a ditch
Action – not a gesture
Says the man who hid inside a fridge

You will not bow to pressure
You will not take the knee
Unless it's to the markets
And hypocrisy

The Little Things That Make You Feel Human Again
#118 / 05:07:2020

July the fourth – Independence Day
We know the virus hasn't gone away
But doors that were locked are opening now
So we'll take care, get through somehow

Glory be – hairdressers at last!
A cut and a chat from a friend in a mask
Ordering food that you haven't prepared
The luxury of an experience shared

Pub doors open – a beer with others
A chat with a stranger, a joke with another
Feels almost normal since I don't know when
The little things that make you feel human again

Blue Sunday
#119 / 05:07:2020

Lock down to lock in – alcohol release
Suddenly we've got a breach of the police

We predict a riot – right on cue
Haven't they got better things to do?

They call it revelry and hi-jinx
Letting off steam, high spirits and drinks

Now we need the boys and girls in blue
Haven't they got better things to do?

The dangerous mix of time plus beer
Would lead to a change in the atmosphere

It all went wrong – well, who knew?!
Haven't they got better things to do?

Nobody wants blue flashing lights
Bottles and flares and drunken fights

We know you've got better things to do
You serve us – we salute you

"Perfectly put." *Janice Johnson*

Happy Birthday And God Bless
#120 / 06:07:2020

Happy birthday – celebrate
Something that is truly great

Those who cure, those who care
Those who shoulder, those who share

Those who listen, those who give
Their lives to help all others live

Those whose patience knows no ends
Those whose patients they call friends

Those who research, those who reach
To share their knowledge when they teach

Those who've been and those who've gone
All who pass that baton on

Those we recognise, front line
Those invisible, behind

All those who we never see
Cleaning floors, making tea

Those who wash or cook the meals
Everyone who turns the wheels

Those who save, those who serve
All of those who so deserve

More than just appreciation
Applause from such a grateful nation

A wage that values contribution
To this living institution

We raise a glass, we all say yes!
Thank you for the NHS

Thank God for – and God bless
Long live our NHS

More Than A Soundtrack

#121 / 07:07:2020
for Ennio Morricone

"Music is an experience, not a science"
So says a maestro
And with your track record
Who are we to argue?

More than just a cowboy theme
You were always better than good
Never bad
And never ever ugly
Not afraid to experiment
Observe, listen, record and evaluate
Patience is a virtuoso
A masterpiece in waiting

The assemblance of sound
The combination of instruments
The accumulation of notes
And the spaces between them
The noise and the silence
The perfect cadence and structure
But what makes it an experience
Is the emotional connection

Art without emotion has no beauty
Music with no feeling does not touch us
Haunting melody, the luminous melancholy
Or quite simply a tune we can whistle
We may not know all your genius
We may not be able to spell your name
But we can all whistle at least one tune
As indeed we are doing right now

Five Lines Of Fun And Truth
#122 / 07:07:2020

The rhyme must always fit the poem
And not vice versa
If you crowbar a rhyme just because it rhymes
It sticks out like a sore thumb and changes the rhythm of the
    line
And makes the poem worser

Shifting The Blame
#123 / 08:07:2020

Shifting the blame – always the same
A quote to confuse and deflect it
Shifting the blame – again and again
To detract, distract, misdirect it

Twisting the blame – it's part of their game
Cowardly, clumsy – at best
Twisting the blame – the lies that remain
Like the truths that remain unconfessed

Twisting the blame with unfounded claims
Yet still, no sign of retraction
Shifting and twisting the blame is their aim
To their own smug satisfaction

Shifting and twisting, resisting all blame
The lines with which they've persisted
No scruples or shame, if it's all the same
We'll blame all you shifty and twisted

Kickstart
#124 / 09:07:2020

It's not that your efforts aren't welcome
But is this where we want to be?
Trying to get back on track
Kickstarting the economy?

Looking for some sort of answer
Returning to normality
Yet still, there are questions of safety
But kickstarting the economy?

A voucher for food on the high street
Reductions on VAT
All very nice – but what is the price
Kickstarting the economy?

These steps may be the direction
To rebuild society
It takes more than cash and injection
To kickstart the economy

Let's kickstart the safety in care homes
The safety of those we can't see
Kickstart the NHS budgets
That's the priority

Economy is just people
Workers like you and like me
It's a kickstart – but it's only a start
If we don't see it through properly

Investment and value and fairness
Quality, equality
All should be taken account of
Kickstarting the economy

Sonnet In Praise Of Creators
#125 / 10:07:2020

Forget not the creators of diversions
Those that lift our spirts and our hearts
In the spotlight or behind the curtains
Appreciate all artists and their arts

The singers of the songs and all the dancers
Those who have the gift for joy and laughter
The writers of the stories that entrance us
Once upon a time – happy ever after

Poets and the playwrights and musicians
Those who paint and sculpt and all the actors
Make belief, reality magicians
Who entertain, inspire – and distract us

Cherish them for bringing us together
For now's the time we need them more than ever

"Phenomenal - you bring a daily bit of sparkle." *Ruth Hilton*

The Name Says It All
#126 / 11:07:2020
for Jack Charlton

Charlton

A word synonymous with football
World Cups and glory

For a certain age
A name that means so much

We may think of Bobby first
But always, always think of Jack in a heartbeat

We may have wanted to play like Bobby
But most of us related to Jack

Endeavour, commitment and fight
We could all be a bit like him

Big Jack at the back – knew his place
Big Jack at the back – did his job

Big Jack at the back – no-one passed
Big Jack at the back – you'd want him on your side

He once said "I couldn't play
But I could stop others playing"

Not true – but true
Uncompromising, straightforward and honest

My dad would always call him "Giraffe neck"
And if dad thought he was "good'un" then he was

In an age where heroes were ordinary
Big Jack was just that – but so much more

One-man club, total legend
Seven hundred and seventy-three appearances

Loved by those who played with him
Loved by those who played for him

The footballer's footballer
Loved by football fans everywhere

Jack Charlton
The name says it all

Mandatory Masks ...
Which Sounds Like It Should Be
A Concept Album Title by Rush
(Which would be more interesting)
#127 / 12:07:2020

Mandatory masks in Morrisons
Mandatory masks in M&S
Mandatory masks?
In shops we ask
Then the answer should be yes

Mandatory masks – a muddled mess
Mixed messages and delays
Mandatory masks?
If so, we ask
Why wait then ten more days?

More than "courtesy and good manners"
Masks are mandatory
It's now time to cover up
Like the ministers in this story

**Sixty (or so) Words And Phrases That Spring To Mind
When Your Football Team Has Been Utterly Embarrassed –
Today It's Everton (3-0 against Wolves, should have been more);
Tomorrow It Could Be Your Team**
#128 / 13:07:2020

Dull and dismal – totally abysmal
Goal-less, guile-less, gut-less and spineless
No formation, no inspiration
No concentration, not even perspiration
Apathetic, non-athletic, pitiful and so pathetic
Useless, toothless – everything but ruthless
Disturbingly disjointed – more than disappointed
Out-muscled, out-tussled, feathers ruffled, out-hustled
No tackle, no bite, no snap, no fight
Boring, clueless – could they really do less?
No show, too slow, never gonna pass go
Leader-less and error strewn
Tortured in the afternoon
Nothing to be proud about
Nothing to be loud about
Nothing we can shout about
Glad there's not a crowd about
Frightened, fearful – you're gonna get an earful
Angry, disgusted, a team that can't be trusted
Utterly, completely, surrendering so meekly
Retreating in defeat-we – do it almost weekly

Heartless – art-less, totally naïve
But still we have faith, still we believe
Hopeless, dopey, the future's looking bleak
Guess what? We'll be back next week

There's A Horse That Bolted Long Ago ...
#129 / 14:07:2020

Why oh why oh why oh why
What are we waiting for?
Why oh why oh why oh why
Delay a little more?

The virus will not go to sleep
Till July twenty-four
There's a horse that bolted long ago
And you can't find the stable door

Why oh why oh why oh why
Must we all endure
This chaos and confusion
And incompetence galore?

Up the creek without a paddle
Never mind an oar
There's a horse that bolted long ago
And you can't find the stable door

Who oh why oh why oh why
Have you chosen to ignore
Warning signs in these plague times
As numbers still they soar?

The scientists are telling us
What horrors lie in store
There's a horse that bolted long ago
And you can't find the stable door

Masks right now just shows quite how
You're drifting from the shore
Floundering and flailing
With every fatal flaw

What is it you cannot see
When we all know the score?
There's a horse that bolted long ago
And you can't find the stable door

Wear A Mask You Idiot –
At Least It'll Cover Up Your Stupid Mouth
#130 / 15:07:2020

Sir Desmond Swayne
A Tory name
Declares his opposition
To shopping guidelines and he claims
Wearing masks is such a pain
And as such he will maintain
This monstrous opposition

On Being Aware
#131 / 16:07:2020

There are books of which I'm aware
In that – I know they are there
Titles of great renown
I'm aware they are around

Aware that they have been written
I read a review with a bit in
Aware of the stories – well, loosely
But the finer details confuse me

Somewhat vague about the chapters
But I think it ends happy ever after
I've seen them on someone else's shelf
But haven't read them myself

There is a reading list
So I am aware that they do exist
I'm aware of all their pages
But reading them takes me ages

Aware, not fully aware – in short
No, I haven't read that report

Effort
#132 / 17:07:2020

Sometimes it's a real effort
To get out of my pyjamas
It hardly seems worth the effort
Unless I'm doing a weekly shop

And when I do get dressed
I seem to be wearing the same clothes
Most days
No reason to do otherwise

Looking in my sock drawer
There are plenty of cheerful colours
But I can't bring myself to wear them
Not in the mood for happy socks

I've come to the conclusion
That I have underpants older than my children
(Probably more supportive and reliable too)
They have seen better days

Then again, so have I
I should really upgrade and buy new
But as someone who shops at Morrisons
Pants with weekly meat and veg doesn't seem right

And hardly worth the effort
Which reminds me
Sometimes it's hardly worth the effort
To get out of these pyjamas and get dressed

A Strong And Sincere Hope
#133 / 18:07:2020

"It is my strong and sincere hope that we will be able to review the outstanding restrictions and allow a more significant return to normality from November at the earliest – possibly in time for Christmas." — Boris Johnson

That Everton will rise again
Invincible in every game
Eclipse past glories with new fame
A strong and sincere hope

That Noddy, Jimmy, Dave and Don
Will reunite for one last song
And once again be number one
A strong and sincere hope

That lottery numbers all come up
England win the next World Cup
A million sales for my next book
A strong and sincere hope

That a cure is found – and fast
Worldwide peace and joy – at last
Poverty is in the past
A strong and sincere hope

That Donald finds humility
Boris finds some honesty
And we all live in harmony
A strong and sincere hope

All the odds against are stacked
None of these are based on fact
Impossible – to be exact
A strong and sincere hope

None of us know what's in store
The future may be insecure
But we deserve so much more
Than a strong and sincere hope

A Sunday Poem
#134 / 19:07:2020

Those like-minded who have chosen to gather
With common spirit who have come together
The sanctity of song
The release of emotion

The unity of public confession
Be it church or chapel of worship
Football ground or sporting occasion
Concert hall, village hall, theatre or pub room

We miss this mass
The coming together of one accord
To share in something special
Capture the spirit within this place

The now that strengthens and uplifts
These moments shared and celebrated
Invisible electricity that connects
Blood and life and breath

Goosebumps, heartbeat and the soul
The sharing of magic
The taking away of inspiration
The fulfilment of unity

Through this
Our common union
This, our holy communion
Peace be with you ...

All We Want For Christmas Is The Vaccine
#135 / 20:07:2020

It may still be the summer
When the skies are clear and blue
And the sun outside is brightly
Shining down on me and you
But we're living in the shadow
Of this COVID-19
And all we want for Christmas is the vaccine

Too far to plan ahead right now
And write a festive list
To share with friends and family
And everyone we've missed
All these season's reasons
Reality or dream?
And all we want for Christmas is the vaccine

Peace on Earth, goodwill to all
And signs that things are better
These, our wishes for the year
Written in a letter
To Santa, God, Buddha, Boris
And everyone between
All we want for Christmas is the vaccine

Never mind the baubles
Never mind the snow
With all this social distancing
Forget the mistletoe
A face mask and some hand gel
And a future that is clean
All we want for Christmas is the vaccine

You Only Get Out …
#136 / 21:07:2020

There's foreign money rushing round
In governmental coffers
Who knows what promises were made
Alongside all these offers?
As the adage goes
It's something or it's nothing
But …
You only get out what you Putin

Capital investments
From these overseas donations?
Kremlin's in the system
Overseeing situations?
Oligarchs – get on your marks
Do they want their own cut in?
Because …
You only get out what you Putin

If you follow all the money
Then you'll always find the truth
But power is corruption
So you'll never find the proof
Investigate these dealings
And the shady doors keep shutting
And …
You only get out what you Putin

"One of the highlights of my day." *Janet New Dubber*

Just Remember This
#137 / 22:07:2020

Believe now all the stories – the Tories voted "yes"
To a deal on the table to sell the NHS

Those who bid the highest are the ones who'll pass the test
Economy, not people but financial interest

National wealth not national health and doing what is best
Don't you dare get ill if you're poor or earning less

This national affrontery, sickening to digest
Believe now all the stories that the Tories voted "yes"

This jewel in our crown that helps those in distress
Pawned and pimped and auctioned, open to contest

Money, spin and mirrors, monopoly and chess
Checkmate and no check-ups, out-manoeuvred in this mess

Just ensure that Trump and all of the US
Are as far away as possible from our NHS

And when we all look back saying "goodnight and God bless"
Just remember this – the Tories voted "yes"

Looking Back
#138 / 23:07:2020

In retrospect
Looking back
I could have written this poem differently

It could have had a better opening line
And a less obvious scheme of rhyme

I could have even
Written every verse in the
Form of a haiku

But did not take the
Time and wasn't prepared to
Do all the planning

I could have edited as I went along
Redrafted and improved
Made it a work in progress

Instead, I responded
With obvious phrases and clichés

Mixing metaphors and ill-thought-out similes
This poem was like a road map of confusion
As easy to follow as dyslexic alphabetti-spaghetti

The inconsistencies in the narrative didn't help
Verses about castles distracted

And because it went on so long
People got bored
This poem became irrelevant
At one point I thought this was the poem
That might change the world

It could have been so different
This poem could have been my legacy

The power and the strength of committed words
Emotion and empathy that reached out
Touched hearts and changed lives

In retrospect
Looking back
I should have written it differently

Settled on a genre
Taken advice from those wiser than me
Learnt from the examples of others
And then created my own masterpiece
Maybe in the highlands

Instead, I often went for cheap jokes
Buffoonery and puns that went from bad to verse
I could have written so much more
And written it so much more betterly
But didn't

What We All Need Now ...
#139 / 24:07:2020

Never mind that food banks are struggling to continue
Never mind that full fat food is always on the menu
Never mind obesity – here's how we can fix it
What we all need now is a fifty-pound voucher bicycle repair kit

Never mind that fast food is so readily available
Never mind the fact it's cheap makes it so retailable
Never mind that quality of life will always take a hit
What we all need now is a fifty-pound voucher bicycle repair kit

Never mind that fruit and veg is costly and expensive
Never mind that changes needed are the most extensive
Never mind all that – let's do a little bit
What we all need now is a fifty-pound voucher bicycle repair kit

Obesity has many forms – economic inequality
Some are fit and some are thin, not just what they want to be
Lose five pounds of weight, get on your bike, get fit
What we all need now is a fifty-pound voucher bicycle repair kit

The Day Of The Mask Parade
#140 / 25:07:2020

The time is now, the day is here
For those who venture far and near
And safety first is crystal clear
In market or arcade
Today's the day but we all know
It should have been this months ago
Government – far too slow
For this mask parade

So … now the science has evolved
Enough for all of those involved
To think the problem could be solved
Opinions have been swayed
Don your mask and off you pop
To the pub or down the shop
Keep on spending, do not stop
In your mask parade

Has common sense prevailed at last?
Or has the time to act fast passed?
The cards are dealt, the die is cast
It seems we've all been played
And now we've found we could be fined
If we leave them all behind
So keep a spare to help remind
You of this mask parade

It's the dithering that's withering
On what you're not delivering
The time you took considering
Decisions to be made
No strategies pinpointed
Responses so disjointed
That left us disappointed
In this mask parade
In this masquerade
To mask your mass charade

Too Long
#141 / 26:07:2020

I haven't spoken to mum
For a while now
Too long

Not seen her since
The day before lockdown
Too long

She's confused
This hasn't helped
Over a hundred miles away

Might as well be the moon
Worlds apart
I'm not sure she understands

Then again
Neither do I
It's been too long

Optimistic Fizz

#142 / 27:07:2020

After Dominic Raab's statement that our PM's "optimistic fizz" would hold the UK together.

What ho! Hoorah! Chin chin!
It's super and it's whizz!
A leader who will lead us with his
Optimistic fizz
Optimistic fizz
Like the bubbles in champagne
That briefly sparkle, rise and pop
Never seen again
The sodastream when drinks are flat
That really is a swizz
Not like on the adverts
Optimistic fizz
The crackle when you try to tune
A radio's what it is
A damp squib of a firework
Optimistic fizz
The buzzing of a buzzer
For an answer in a quiz
That you thought was right but isn't
Optimistic fizz
Retro aftershave
To get the ladies in a tizz
Who needs Hai Karate when there's
Optimistic Fizz?
The right man for the job?
The bee's knees and the biz?
Or a snake oil selling salesman and his
Optimistic Fizz?
We need statesmanship, thoroughness, respectability
Gravitas, seriousness and diplomacy
Alas – all these won't come to pass
Not qualities of his
Just effervescent emptiness
And optimistic fizz

Coronavee The Mystery Cat

#143 / 28:07:2020

Written after it was confirmed that a cat had contracted COVID-19 – with apologies to T.S. Eliot.

Coronavee the hidden cat that no-one ever sees
Coronavee the mystery cat who's bound to make you sneeze

He's the bafflement of doctors and scientists despair
For when they try to find him – Coronavee's not there

Coronavee's the cat amongst the pigeons of us all
This feline leaves us feline not so well and rather small

You may see him in the market, you may see him in the square
But when you try to stop him – Coronavee's not there

Coronavee, Coronavee – there's no-one like Coronavee
Coronavee – a loner – he – can spread diseases easily

You may hear a little mewling or a distant sort of purr
But wherever you are looking Coronavee's not there

Coronavee's the secret kitty we all know is there
Maybe in the basement or maybe on the stair

Far too clever to be found by likes of you and me
The one and only viral cat that is Coronavee!

Situation Vacant
#144 / 29:07:2020

Situation Vacant – and has been for some time
Situation Vacant – sign on the dotted line
Opportunity is knocking – open up the door
If you have the qualities that we are looking for ...
Wanted:
Can you speak in sentences
On a daily basis?
Charismatic with one of
Those camera-friendly faces?
Someone who's appealing
To all women and all men
Can you be the spokesperson
For those in Number Ten?
Someone analytical
Partisan political
Toe the party line and then
Mouth the words for Number Ten
Thick of skin, committed, bold
To only do what they are told
Stand and face the nation's press
Don't say no and don't say yes
Someone sharp of tongue and wit
Who understands the game
Someone who can answer questions
Directly while deflecting blame
Someone calming, non-alarming
Cool and quite collected
Unflustered and un-blustered
Someone unelected
Somebody convincing
Can lie without the wincing
Can you think while on your feet?
Unlike those in Downing Street
Take the bullets when they're fired
Do all this – then you'll be hired
All for a hundred grand a year
Applications wanted here

Second
#145 / 30:07:2020

Second's out
Second spike
People doing
What they like
Second wave
Second thought
Not doing
What we ought
Second half
Second guess
Second rate
Total mess
Second class
Second to none
Got it wrong
All along
Second chance
Not quite
Wish we had
Second sight

The Greatest Tory Ever Sold
#146 / 31:07:2020

The Bible says
Honour thy father and mother
I've changed it a bit
To honour my brother
All these commandments
From way back in time
They're so out of date
I much prefer mine

Distant
#147 / 01:08:2020

The farce that city pubs and bars
Exist with no resistance
Where masses gather freely
To drink with great persistence
Yet you cancel Eid by Twitter feed
From an anti-social distance
Insensitive at best – but ...
As usual – inconsistent

Sunday
#148 / 02:08:2020

Today, being Sunday
And traditionally being a "day of rest"
There will be no poem
Save these few words
As a child
Sundays meant church three times
No playing out down the rec
And limited television
Sunday
A day of rest
A family day
A day to pray
Today then
It is much the same
As I say a little prayer for our family
And prepare to drive to mum's
The rest of the world can wait
The rest of the week can wait
The rest of my list of things to do can wait
Today – a day of rest

**The Inevitability Upon Driving To Lancashire
To See Mum After Four Months Of Lockdown**
#149 / 03:08:2020

Inevitably there were tears
Inevitably we couldn't resist the need to embrace
Inevitably we felt guilty and awkward in the current climate
Inevitably we drove past crowded beer gardens
Where people neither felt guilty or awkward, inevitably

Noises Off
#150 / 04:08:2020

There's a tap-dancing albatross on my roof
Not really
Although I haven't actually checked
But it's a good opening line for a poem

Awoken early, very early
By noises off that sound like the above
Either that or the mice have hobnail boots
And are playing football with a crab apple
Early morning house silence amplifies all sound
As the squirrel with a lump hammer
Adjusts the chimney breast
And rearranges several tiles
Maybe it's not actually outside …
Perhaps there's a party in the loft
And headbanging bats are bouncing off beams
While biting the heads off jelly babies
A cup of tea later
The noises have stopped
The house has woken
And I have this poem

I go outside to welcome the day
Look up
An albatross flies off
Tap-dancing shoes fall with a percussive flourish

Early
#151 / 05:08:2020

In my back garden
The early birds are catching worms
Two magpies, a baby blackbird
And a sparrow to be exact

At the kitchen table
The early poet has finished in the bathroom
Had two rounds of toast
And is on his second cup of tea

He is also admiring his shed
The one he painted yesterday
While listening to Test Match Special
"Willow" to be exact – or light green

There is paint left over
So he is considering painting the gate
The same shade of light green
Waste not want not eh?

The early poet is catching words
And just like the paint pot
There are some left over …
Save them for another poem

Public Service Broadcasting
#152 / 06:08:2020

Are you over seventy-five?
Isolated? Alone? Worried? Confused? In need of company?
Something to watch to while away the hours?
Good. We are here. However, because of COVID-19
We have no new programmes to speak of
Except the news of course – we are very good at that
And the news is this: Now your TV licence is no longer free
Bring Back Cash – Business Before Customers

To Be Continued
#153 / 07:08:2020
A lyric for a song released on this date by Don Powell's Occasional Flames
– reached No. 90 in the iTunes chart and is still available to download.

All the poems I nearly wrote
All those words stuck in my throat
Every scribbled, misspelled note
To be continued

All the novels that I'd planned
With characters you can understand
Fifty pages later and
To be continued

All the paintings that I'd start
Original, unique and smart
Possibly great works of art
To be continued

All responsibility –
creatively diminished
All potential masterpieces
To be continued

Everything is all in place
And if I let it go to waste
Losing pace, losing face
To be continued

It's time to take my chances now
Put the work in and somehow
See it through and take a bow
To be continued

I'm putting off today and thinking about tomorrow
What could have been
What should have been
Which ideas I'm to follow
I should be full to bursting but I'm empty and I'm hollow

Part-Time Pop Star
#154 / 08:08:2020

Peaked at number ninety
Hovered around the hundred mark
All day and all of the night
Part-time pop stars

At one point wedged between
Mariah and Beyoncé
Oh … if only …
Part-time pop stars

Not bad for three old farts
And a glam rock pensioner
Messing about on social media
Part-time pop stars

Today – iTunes
Tomorrow – oblivion
The day after – a cup of tea and a biscuit
Part-time pop stars

Still available
As the song says
'To Be Continued'
Part-time pop stars

Today Has Not Been A Day For Poetry
#155 / 09:08:2020

Today has not been a day for poetry
It has been a day for sorting the garage out
Of course, the garage has no car in it
Boxes and bags, assorted tools, bikes and … stuff

Boxes we haven't opened since we moved in
All those years ago
Bits of wood and wire that I thought might come in handy
But haven't

Although if I throw them away today
I'll no doubt need them tomorrow
Two carrier bags full of handwritten cassette tapes
That I'll never play but are full of memories

Paint I can't remember buying or using
That no longer resembles the shade on the tin anyway
Stuff, just chucked in there
Out of sight and out of mind

Until today
Today has not been a day for poetry
But Jenga with garage detritus
Rubbish has been chucked

The tumble drier has been moved
As have three bikes, one mower
Bin bags, boxes and assorted tools
All assigned new positions

Still accessible but more compact
And – with it being Sunday –
It seems it is a day of miracles …
The car is now inside the garage

I'm Getting To Quite Like My Mask
#156 / 10:08:2020

Now that you come to ask
It's not such an onerous task
You can't hear me grumble
Just a faint mumble
I'm getting to quite like my mask

When those in the street try to pass
Too rudely, too close and too fast
They don't hear the swearing
Beneath what I'm wearing
I'm getting to quite like my mask

I may look like a social outcast
But I've found a bright side – at last
No chance of lip readin'
There's a strange freedom
I'm getting to quite like my mask

Fifty–Bloody–Nine
#157 / 11:08:2020

So, I'm nearly sixty
Fifty – bloody – nine
And that is nearly SIXTY!

My maths is not deserting me
Even in these seemingly advancing years
Yes, fifty-nine

And I'm framing fifteen-pence Slade posters
From 1973 or something mad like that
Framing them!

They were never allowed on my bedroom walls at home
Mum said they would ruin the wallpaper
Dad just said they were rubbish

They briefly adorned college walls
As a statement of commitment, irony
And the fact that I could

College feels like the recent past by the way
But is nearly forty years ago
How did that happen?

Back to the Slade posters ...
They have NEVER – and I mean – NEVER
Appeared on any interior household wall during
Thirty years of married life

But now, I have a den
A room in the garage
Not in the house
And not a comment on the marriage either

It used to be my son's bolthole
PlayStation, music, cigarettes
Etcetera ...
And we all know about the etcetera ...
But now, it's been fumigated
Reclaimed, repainted, fumigated
Rearranged, fumigated
And it's mine

Desk, computer, bookshelves and books
Old magazines, concert programmes
Music, several ukuleles
And a settee – doubly fumigated

And here I am writing, typing
Creating and curating, reading, listening, hiding ...
Surrounded by a few of my favourite things
Things – my favourite people are in the house

Fifty-nine
My Slade posters are framed
They won't ruin any wallpaper
And they never were rubbish

Not An Invasion
#158 / 12:08:2020

We found them on our beaches
We found them on our sands

They came across our waters
They came from distant lands

They didn't come with malice
Or detailed battle plans

They didn't come with treaties
Ultimatums and demands

They didn't come with guns
Or weapons in their hands

They came with all the problems
We do not understand

They came with desperation
Nothing underhand

In fact they came with nothing
Each woman, child and man

An invitation-less visit ...
But ... it's not an invasion though, is it?

Whatever it is, this situation
Whatever it is, it's not an invasion

Take that etymology from the equation
Not an assault or attack on our nation

No onslaught that's evil or sly infiltration
No violent offensive and no violation

Maybe an act of sheer desperation
Whatever it is, it's not an invasion

Let's be clear and explicit
That's not an invasion though, is it?

Watch, This Pace …
#159 / 13:08:2020

Today I put my watch back on
For the first time since my own lockdown
145 days
3480 hours
208,800 minutes
12528000 seconds
Not that I've been counting
As I haven't had my watch on
I'm not even sure what the last number is
Just a number on a calculator screen
Which some readers may even go
And double-check …
My wrist feels burdened, heavier
But it feels like it's time to move on
Reclaim some sense of normal
Even though it is clearly not the case
We have holiday weather
Feels like we are abroad
Our outlook reflects this
We are carefree – apart from shopping masks
Pubs are getting fuller
Attitudes more blasé
Social distancing is fluid and elastic
Yet there is still a death toll
Still, it feels like time to put my watch back on
Tomorrow, I may even open my diary
Although its blank pages where work once lived
Will be difficult to look at

A Statement From The Department Of Education
On Behalf Of The Government
#160 / 14:08:2020

Never mind the experts
Who've taught and made their mark
We know what's best to pass the test
So we'll tear it all apart
We don't want double standards
It's perfect common sense
We don't want those promoted beyond their competence

Never mind the lockdown
The problems and pandemic
Never mind that policies
Affect the academic
Never mind the work achieved
The stress that is immense
We don't want those promoted beyond their competence

Never mind the changing world
And everything uncertain
Never mind the best laid plans
Never mind the hurting
Never mind all that at all
It's our experience
We don't want those promoted beyond their competence

This isn't just a random act
But a strategy to show
We safeguard our society
Preserve the status quo
Harrow, Eton – won't be beaten
Here's the recompense
We can't have those promoted beyond their competence

Knowledge isn't privilege
It should not be a shield
To keep all those from entering
A level playing field

Equal opportunities
Not locked gates and a fence
But we can't have those promoted beyond their competence

Just look at all we've done
We know you'll all agree
All the waste on track and trace
The millions on PPE
And so much more that we've ignored
We are the evidence
Of people being promoted beyond their competence

We know it's true, we know we're right
There is no pretence
We are those promoted beyond our competence

"Robust Results"
#161 / 15:08:2020

Robust results – yet standards are raided
Eton and Harrow will not be downgraded
Boundaries change as lines become shaded
Eton and Harrow will not be downgraded
Teachers' predictions are changed and then traded
Eton and Harrow will not be downgraded
Recommendations ignored and blockaded
Eton and Harrow will not be downgraded
Dreams have been shattered, hopes have all faded
Eton and Harrow will not be downgraded
Depressed and downhearted, frustrated and jaded
Eton and Harrow will not be downgraded
Are we convinced? Are we persuaded?
Eton and Harrow will not be downgraded
The truth is the truth that can't be evaded
Eton and Harrow will not be downgraded

The Algorhythm Method
#162 / 16:08:2020

Today's poem has been adversely affected
By current circumstances
It was to be a much longer and adventurous poem
But has been edited to much less than its original vision

Not only that
But the *A B A B* rhyme scheme
That was to be deployed
Has now been rearranged imperceptibly

Apparently, there is nothing to be done
There are no Poetry Police
No *Serious Rhyme Squad*
Who can take this matter up

It would seem that poetic license has been revoked
And instead, there is this
Where whatever ending or punchline was in mind
Has been withdrawn, prematurely

Thanks to the algorhythm method

Put The Answers Right

#163 / 17:08:2020

After Lord Baker of Dorking advised: "If you are in a hole, stop digging."

The calculations that you made
Are neither fair nor just
The figures you configured
Just lead to more mistrust

If you're in a hole, stop digging
It's clear as day and night
Hold your hands up – just say sorry
Put the answers right

This chaos you created
This devastating mess
Where just what happens next
Is anybody's guess

If you're in a hole, stop digging
Look up to the light
Put down your spades, raise those grades
And put the answers right

Everybody knows it's wrong
It's obvious and clear
If it was a football match
VAR is here

If you're in a hole stop digging
You can't win a losing fight
Don't attack – just backtrack
And put the answers right
You're digging your own graves
For the next election
This generation won't forget
Your un-natural selection

If you're in a hole stop digging
Before you're out of sight
Don't tell lies – apologise
And put the answers right

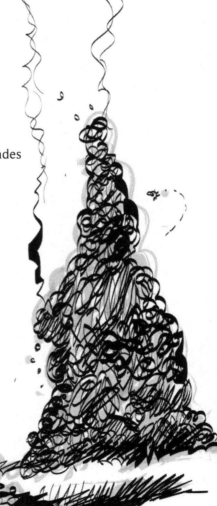

U Turn
#164 / 18:08:2020

You turned against the teachers
And all their expertise
You turned against the pupils
In difficult days like these
You turned against opinion
Of varying degrees
You turned – you turned – you turned
You turned opportunity
To failure not success
You turned this situation
Into un-needed stress
You turned down a chance
To do just what is best
You turned – you turned – you turned
You turned up the heat
When you could have turned it down
You turned education
Into a battleground
You turned this can of worms
Upside down and on the ground
You turned – you turned – you turned
You turned your backs on many
And chose to face the few
Now you want to turn the tide
In what you seek to do
Turn back time to change your lies
Into something true
You turned – you turned – you turned
Utterly Unfeeling
Unacceptable at best
Untrustworthy Undone
Untenable Unimpressed
Unelectable and Useless
Ungraded in this test
U failed – U failed – U failed

Prayer For The Day
#165 / 19:08:2020

May today be the day
Where hopes and dreams come true

May today be the day
Where things work out for just for you

May today be the day
That's filled with joy, not fears

May today be the day
That has no need for tears

May efforts all be recognised
Achievements celebrated

Due diligence rewarded
Paths illuminated

May today just be that day
Where the passed stay passed and so

You're looking to the future
On your marks, get set, go!

Dear Gavin
#166 / 20:08:2020

It can't have been a surprise
It's not a bolt from the blue
It's been on the cards for months now
But what did you do?
Just where was your planning?
Where was your preparation?
Your revision and working out
For this examination?

You knew this date was coming
You could have done much more
But left it all last minute
And panicked on the night before
Then realised you'd get things wrong
And without a second glance
Cancelled and delayed it all
To give yourself a second chance

Ill-prepared ineptitude
You failed at every stage
You really must try harder
If you're going to make up grades
But despite the facts in black and white
Don't worry about the shouting mob
You're with the rest who fail each test
You too can keep your job

"I've looked forward to reading your poems every morning."
Nomis Simon Baurley

Tom Sawyer, A Girl Called Eddy And A Boy Called Bill
#167 / 21:08:2020

'Huckleberry Unfinished'
Was going to be the witty title for this poem
As yesterday was spent painting a fence

Except it was Tom Sawyer
And he whitewashed a fence
Whereas mine is "Urban Slate" – or grey, as I like to call it

And the job is incomplete
Hence 'Huckleberry Unfinished'

Talking of names
I was joined by A Girl Called Eddy
And a boy called Bill

Companions throughout the day
I sang along to heartbreak songs
And imagined playing guitar on 'Jets at Dawn'

Should the weather be acceptable
We will reconvene, the three of us
With the "Urban Slate"

Or in this garden
"Suburban Slade"

An Important Question In The Form Of A Haiku Regarding My Daily Task
#168 / 22:08:2020

a poem to write
a fence to paint – which to fin
-ish first ... the poem

COVID Whispers
#169 / 23:08:2020

Shush … I haven't gone away
I haven't disappeared
Still lurking, doing my dirty work
I'm … still … here

I may not be the front page news
Like earlier in the year
But silence is my strength and power
I'm … still … here

Because you all want to return
To all that you hold dear
Normality is mine
I'm … still … here

You may be bored or weary
Forgotten all your fear
Take all the risks you want
I'm … still … here

Ambivalence – my ally
To help me stay so near
Your laziness – my friend
I'm … still … here

Rave on, relax, distract yourself
But let's be crystal clear
Wherever you go, whatever you do
I'll be waiting just for you
I'm … still … here

A Breath Of Fresh Air
#170 / 24:08:2020

With my first cup of tea
I stand outside my back door

Amongst other things
I admire my newly painted fence

The one that my daughter says
"Makes the grass look greener"

The wind whispers I know not what
But it is soothing

An arrogant magpie struts
One for sorrow – not as soothing

The wind, the fence, the magpie and me
And my first cup of tea

I will try to savour this moment
This peace for as long as possible

The wind may indeed whisper
But it does not lie

"A real boost to my day." *Keith Powell*

We Only Really Know Two Lines
#171 / 25:08:2020

Great tune, rousing finale
Gets the pulses racing
A national anthem – but better
Not sure about the words though
Don't know them all, or understand them
But those I do, I sing along with
Well, the chorus …
Don't really want to rule the waves
Don't believe in slavery
Don't believe in making slaves of others
Britain first at heaven's command
Not bothered about native oaks
Chest-beating, flag-waving, inflated pride
And national glory at the expense of others
Not really my thing
Not that we shouldn't celebrate nationality
Lots we can be proud about
Time to reclaim the Union Jack
What a tune though!
What atmosphere and passion!
Maybe it's time to rewrite the words …

"Excellent - hits the spot." *Deirdre Speed*

And I Thought "Mutant Algorithm"
Was The Latest Album By Radiohead ...
#172 / 26:08:2020

Just don't blame the government
It's not our fault this time
We are the not the cause
Of this heinous cybercrime
And it wasn't OFQAL either
Who turned those grades from A to D
You can blame the mutant algorithm
Just don't blame me

This algorithm's deadly
And its dangerous mutation
Threatening our world
Infecting education
Science fiction turns to fact
The evidence is here to see
You can blame the mutant algorithm
Just don't blame me

This beast is out of control
A law unto itself
Constantly evolving
This monster's something else
Once a number programme
Now a living entity
You can blame the mutant algorithm
Just don't blame me

This raging mass of numbers
These codes that ever spiral
These matrix calculations
This evil that is viral
This silent violent predator
This unseen enemy
You can blame the mutant algorithm
Just don't blame me

It's really, really, really real
Not something we've made up
To cloud the fact we got it wrong
And put your grades back up
But somehow this thing escaped
From a strange laborat'ry
You can blame the mutant algorithm
Just don't blame me

It Don't Mean A Thing If It Ain't Got That Swing
#173 / 27:08:2020

The Burnley Express
Jimmy Anderson – King of Swing
Unassuming hero
Ultimate professional
Metronomic guile
Fast but not furious
Intelligence and pace
Controlled aggression
Leader of the attack
Leader of the pack
Leader by example
Living legend who leads the way
Opening act yet top of the bill
Bag of tricks, sleight of hand
Twenty-two-yard magician
Wizard in dizzying spells
Mister More-than-Reliable
Numbers speak for themselves
Six hundred Test Match wickets
And still counting
The Burnley Express
Always on time
Always on the right tracks
Not over yet
Mister Anderson sir
We salute you

That Greenbelt Festival Feeling
#174 / 28:08:2020

August Bank Holiday weekend
And normally I'd be scratching that Greenbelt itch

At this point for the last forty-plus years
I would have been somewhere in a festival field
Celebrating friends and extended family
That once-a-year faithful gathering

But not today
Not me
Not any of us
Not this year when we probably need it most

I'm home with a cup of tea in hand
Looking out of the window at the pouring rain
Thinking of those annual connections
The inspiration and encouragement
The special place and special people

Fellowship of friendship
Affirmation of faithfulness
Communion of kindred spirits
The challenge of the new
Amongst the traditions of the old

So many magical moments
So many pivotal times
So many special people
Beautiful humans

The songs of those newly discovered
Who become lifelong friends
Lifelong friends and open hearts
Open hearts and restless souls
Restless souls and questions asked
Questions asked and answers offered
Answers offered and memories shared
Memories shared and cups of tea
Cups of tea and ...

Cups of tea and I'm at home
Looking at the rain
Partly glad I'm warm and safe and dry
But mostly wishing I was there and wet
Soaked in the joy of my Greenbelt gathering

Until next year my friends
Until next year
I'll put the kettle on
And think of you all and smile

Daily Prayer
#175 / 29:08:2020

Answers for the questions
Not yet asked
Solutions to problems
So far un-encountered
Respite from these burdens
Carried round so long
Strength for the weaknesses
That bring us to our knees

Wisdom and timing
To do just what is right
Grace to accept
All that is past and gone
Forgiveness to give
Healing to share
Peace in the storm
That never seems to cease

Comfort for the heart
Fragile and breaking
Solace for the soul
Troubled and alone
Sunshine for the day
Calm for the night
Belief that tomorrow
Can be a better day

Hand-Sized Biting Spiders In Your Home ...
And They're Looking For Sex!
#176 / 30:08:2020
This was an actual headline!

There's a danger that is stranger than the truth
Amorous arachnids are descending from the roof
Guaranteed revulsion – to make you nervous wrecks
Hand-sized biting spiders in your home ... and they're looking for sex!

Don't be left alone when inside your empty room
Turn on all your lights and illuminate the gloom
Look behind each cushion, be careful with your checks
Hand-sized biting spiders in your home ... and they're looking for sex!

Fatal when they mate – beware of that attraction
You'll get so much more than a chemical reaction
Taken unawares, beware the side-effects
Hand-sized biting spiders in your home ... and they're looking for sex!

So seal up all the buttons on your shirts and on your blouses
Check the sheets and pillows in the bedrooms of your houses
Sellotape into your socks, the legs of all your kecks
Hand-sized biting spiders in your home ... and they're looking for sex!

If you feel a tickle that is rising near your thigh
Do not scream or groan – and certainly don't sigh
Some things will start to shrink as others start to flex
Hand-sized biting spiders in your home ... and they're looking for sex!

These eight-legged groove machines, these arthropods on heat
These swingers on their threads of lust spinning their deceit
More than just a love-bite when they peck upon your necks
Hand-sized biting spiders in your home ... and they're looking for sex!

Action first and fast when they start to manoeuvre
Be ready with the feather duster, ready with the hoover
Decisive and incisive – ensure they'll be an ex
Hand-sized biting spiders in your home ... and they're looking for sex!

Friends In A Field
#177 / 31:08:2020

Friends in a field
I have missed you
More than you can know

Lifelong histories and open hearts
Open arms and listening ears
Raucous laughter and a thousand cups of tea

Friends in a field
I have missed you
Familiar faces and kindred spirits

That field where dreams take shape
That field where souls are stirred
That field of heavenly dew

Friends in a field
Our annual family gathering
Forty-plus years of faith and fellowship

Pilgrims and travellers
At the heart of the covenant
With the art of the covenant

Yes, there is the music
And yes, there are the talks
But I think we'd all still meet if not

For we are the people
We are the festival
We are so much more than just

Friends in a field

New
#178 / 01:09:2020

New term
New school year
New routines
New ideas
New rules
New days
New systems
New ways
New worries
New stress
New confusion
New tests
New rooms
New signs
New work
New times
New me
New you
New beginnings
All new

A Little Patience
#179 / 02:09:2020

A little patience
To get things just right
A little patience
As new ways are trialled
A little patience
From the pupils
A little patience
From the teachers
A little patience
From the parents
A little patience
From everyone
A little patience
To work things out
A little patience
To keep things as safe as possible
And hopefully
A little patience
Means
No little patients

Public Enema
#180 / 03:09:2020

COVID-19
Already unclean
Finding new methods to use
To spread its infection
In every direction
Wafting through pipes and up through your loos

Surfing in cisterns
And round drainage systems
Surviving the effluent ooze
Beats toilet brushes
Fighting the flushes
Wafting through pipes and up through your loos

This enemy – public
Number one – double it
Worse than the worst number twos
You can't see it coming
Invading your plumbing
Wafting through pipes and up through your loos

It will rise and ascend
From behind your U-bend
Ignoring the don'ts and the dos
However you soil it
Escaping your toilet
Wafting through pipes and up through your loos

Yes, COVID-19
In every latrine
Its tactics are meant to confuse
Craftily wafting
And draughtily drafting
Right through the pipes and up through your loos

Black And White
#181 / 03:09:2020

There are two magpies in my garden
They haven't heard the news
Or read the script
There is no joy

Oblivious to any bigger picture
They are merely early birds
Searching for worms
Trying to stay alive

Still they find the time to sing

One Hundred And Fifty-Five Days
#182 / 04:09:2020

One hundred and fifty-five days
Since I last went out to work

As in out
Out of the house
To somewhere else

One hundred and fifty-five days
Since I last faced an audience

As in live
There in front of me
Not on a Zoom screen

So here I am
Not thinking tee-shirts

But a real shirt with buttons
Trousers and actual shoes
Not slippers

I've missed my work
More than I know

The interaction, the laughter
Of audience and performer
When poetry truly lives

One hundred and fifty-five days
And I'm truly looking forward to this

Let's hope and pray that it is not
One hundred and fifty-five days
Before I get to do it all again

**Nine Lines Of An Average Nature
In Order To Reach A Suitable Pun**
#183 / 05:09:2020

Just who is that masked man
Friend or foe or stranger
Wanting us to follow and
Wear masks to ward of danger?

Or does the mask disguise the sham
That when it all hits the fan
And we're indebted to his plan
Everyone is cap in hand
To – The Loan Arranger

The Elephant In The Room
#184 / 06:09:2020

The elephant in the room
Grows bigger day by day
The elephant in the room
That will not go away
We may have been distracted
For the best part of a year
But the mess that is Brexit is still here

The elephant in the room
Not silent for much longer
Its presence unavoidable
And influence much stronger
Murky waters muddier
Nothing crystal clear
And the mess that is Brexit is still here

The elephant in the room
That has slumbered in this past
Has lumbered into life
And is waking up at last
Minimal discussions
Repercussions that we fear
And the mess that is Brexit is still here

The elephant in the room
Has realised the powers
That could be unleashed
From its ivory towers
We could be trampled underfoot
Confusion far and near
And the mess that is Brexit is still here

No Surprise
#185 / 07:09:2020

Normality – mortality
Another number dies
And still we are ambivalent
The numbers start to rise

We seem to have forgotten
The guideline still applies
Blasé in the bars and shops
Numbers start to rise

However much you spin it
There's no way to disguise
The answers lie unfound
As the numbers start to rise

We may watch it all unfold
Before our very eyes
But it doesn't seem to register
That numbers start to rise

Negligent – not vigilant
So it can't be a surprise
That here we are again
And still the numbers rise

Recipe For Disaster
#186 / 08:09:2020

This "OVEN READY DEAL"
This soundbite that you've chosen
This turkey's past its sell by date
Plus the fact – it's frozen

The Joy Of Six
#187 / 09:09:2020

Be careful how you gather
Be careful where you mix
It's the magic number
With the joy of six

You won't get your highs
You won't get your kicks
On route – or en suite
With the joy of six

Certainly no Boogie Nights
And no Ballroom Blitz
More Saturday Night Fever
With the joy of six

Less than five – stay alive
More and COVID sticks
Seven isn't heaven …
The joy of six

Act Fast?
#188 / 10:09:2020

Hands – Face – Space
Our brave Prime Minister speaks
We must act fast to save lives ...
Starting from next week

I wobble and I waddle when I walk
I want to be slim and oh so sleek
Act fast – time to diet
I think I'll start next week

There's a smell of effluence
With no paddle – up this creek
Act fast – SOS
Send a message out next week

There's a fire in the house
I smell the smoke and I feel the heat
Act fast – call the fire brigade
And then they can come next week

Like the Titanic and the iceberg
There seems to be a little leak
Act fast – get the lifeboats
Starting from next week

Coronavirus crisis rises
Still the numbers yet to peak
Act fast – save lives
Starting from next week

Pig's Ear, Dog's Dinner
#189 / 11:09:2020

Trade deal renegations
The hoo-ha that's in Brussels
Non negotiations
Confusing verbal tussles
Michael waves his Union Jack
And tries to flex his muscles

There's talk of cheese and chicken
Arguments on cod
Orders re soft borders
And other things most odd
Who will buy and when and why
And who will give the nod

"Trust and confidence are key"
To unlock any door
Significant differences remain
On what we're looking for
Britannia waives the rules
And sings of sovereign law

Like knitting with blancmange
Or trying to juggle with jelly
This no deal wheeler-dealing
Has left this ship unsteady
Pig's ear, dog's dinner
Far from oven ready

We get what we deserve – if we voted *Yes*
Receive our just desserts – with this Eton Mess
Led by this buffoon – failing to impress
Babbling buffoon or baffling baboon – same thing I guess

Some People Are On the Pitch ...
#190 / 12:09:2020

As football kicks off once again
The grounds are empty, now, as then
Just the sound of these few men
No volume, roar or row
We dreamed of stadia full of crowds
But alas, it's not allowed
We thought it was all over
                              ... It isn't now

Instead we fans are far away
Wishing we were there today
Watching all our heroes play
And cheer along, somehow
Instead there's just the joy of six
In front of our TV sets
We thought it was all over
                              ... It isn't now

Looking forward to the action
Football is the main attraction
Any positive distraction
COVID will allow
Sick of all this quarantine
We just want our football team
We thought it was all over
                              ... It isn't now

It may just be a football match
A ninety-minute escape hatch
One game at once and after that
We don't know why or how
All of this will ever end
And will things be the same again?
We thought it was all over
                              ... It isn't now

**I'm Not Used To Writing Optimistic Poems After
The First Game Of A New Football Season With Everton**
#191 / 13:09:2020

Same shirt – different team
Same team – different game
Same game – different football
Same football – different result

New season – old ambitions
New ambitions – old goals
New goals – old traditions
New traditions – old master

Rejected By Morrisons
#192 / 14:09:2020

That Morrisons job – long since rejected
Failed application – never selected

Time on my hands, once unexpected
A daily routine – long since neglected

A poem a day – a routine perfected
About the infected and all those affected

Or feeling let down by those we elected
A diary of thoughts and feelings dissected

All the poems later – shared and connected
Two books and counting – verses collected

Morning Moments
#193 / 15:09:2020

Were I braver and less inhibited
I would stride naked in my garden
The soles of my feet
Absorbing the life-dew diamond sheen

Days like these are numbered
Autumn temperatures will soon fall
It could be a last chance
To feel soothing sunshine warm my skin

However, being inhibited
And of a certain age and weight
The best I can do is walk to the bins
In my flip-flops and dressing gown

The sun still feels, soothes
And were the dew diamonds
Richness would be mine forever
Rather than just these morning moments

Plus, there's the neighbours to consider
Wouldn't want to traumatise them

You Give Incompetence A Bad Name
#194 / 16:09:2020

Unprecedented – maybe, but now it's been so long
We've had this situation and still you get it wrong
Not a trace of track and trace and you won't take the blame
You give incompetence a bad name

Every day's the same – you huffing, puffing, bluffing
When all is said and done – it all adds up to nothing
Hello darkness my old friend – here we are again
You give incompetence a bad name

Promises and policies – from when you were elected
The goalposts have been moved – just as we expected
The Brexit exit voted just hasn't stayed the same
You give incompetence a bad name

Bereft of moral fibre and bereft of any vision
The inconsistencies to stick to a decision
A catalogue of chances missed exist to prove this claim
You give incompetence a bad name

What next for Great Britain? We haven't got a clue
Bad news for everyone – the same is true of you
In conclusion, more confusion destined to remain
You give incompetence a bad name

Not A Trace
#195 / 17:09:2020

Let's all go to Telford
Bolton to Inverness
Not a trace of track and trace
No sign of a test

Seven weeks on Thursday
Ten thirty-five is best
Not a trace of track and trace
Cancelling the test

A pandemic that is national
North, south, east and west
Not a trace of track and trace
Try to find a test

It's not like it's surprising
So why this useless mess?
Not a trace of track and trace
No chance of a test

You can travel far and wide
Scour every single place
Discover this green pleasant land
Not a trace of track and trace

How're You Doing?
#196 / 18:09:2020

Well – you know
Good days and bad days
Actually – not true
No good days
Mostly indifferent days
Where every day feels like yesterday
And there is no new tomorrow

Sometimes a friend might ring
Or an exciting email pops up
Occasionally an interesting thread
Might distract for a while on social media
But
Mostly
It's
Boring
Or
Worse

So …
How am I doing?
Well
I'm not dead from COVID-19
But I may be dying a little bit inside
Every
Single
Day

Ode To Jacob
#197 / 19:09:2020

Oh Jacob how we've missed you
Your endless carping on
About our government so great
And the work that they have done

Oh Jacob how we've missed you
Like a soldier in our trenches
Your tireless contribution
Reclining on our benches

Oh Jacob how we've missed you
And your national civic duty
Like Beano's Walter the Softy
Mutating with Lord Snooty

Oh Jacob how we've missed you
Your verbal cut and thrust
That narrow-minded bigotry
That's gained you so much trust

Oh Jacob how we've missed you
Your willingness to blame
And how your "Christian views"
Give Jesus a bad name

Oh Jacob how we've missed you
You contribute so much
Out of time and out of step
And always out of touch

Better Get Things Ready For Locktober
#198 / 20:09:2020

The numbers do not lie, there in black and white
Second wave, second spike, call it what you like
We won't be going anywhere until this is all over
Better get things ready for Locktober

Positively negative, it's getting worse again
Prepare the way for curfews and further COVID pain
I feel the need to drink a lot but maybe should stay sober
Better get things ready for Locktober

Self-isolation stakes – or there's a price to pay
With health and wealth so treat yourself and stay at home each
day
No more tours to castles, no more the wild rover
Better get things ready for Locktober

No end in sight – it's just going on forever
We'd like to hope and pray that we'll get through this together
Don't know when – we'll meet again – maybe by cliffs at Dover
Better get things ready for Locktober

We Must All Have The Ability To Disagree Politely
#199 / 20:09:2020

You are all my friends
That is why we are here
There are connections
Some old, some new
But you are all connections

You are all my friends
Yet we may see things differently
Very differently at times
But that should not be a reason
For unnecessary rudeness

Not every poem I write is the truth
Sometimes just a pun, a joke
Or stretching the truth to make a point
Just an opinion

Opinions are there to be challenged
Your opinion may differ
My opinion may clash
But at the end of the day
They are opinions

You are all my friends
And if we must disagree
Let us do so with politeness
Humour and respect
Without condescension or personal attack

Poem Two Hundred
#200 / 21:09:2020

Two hundred poems
Who would have thought
That when all this started
I would have two hundred poems to show for it?

Not all good poems
Obviously
But all of them a response – at the time
And all of them honest – at the time

I keep thinking
That there'll be nothing more to write about
That it's all been said before
Then the gift that unfortunately keeps on giving

Gives again

Oh the irony
As "he" worries about money
It would be funny
If it was so hideously and seriously offensive

Unemployed, minimum wage, furloughed, ill …
And "he" worries about hiring a nanny
Apparently, according to an un-named source
He "doesn't seem to enjoy being at the helm in rough seas"

At last
We have something in common

The Nation Watched
#201 / 22:09:2020

The Prime Minister did his best
While everyone waited for Bake Off

The country is in crisis
But we'd rather have Bake Off

It's time to get really serious about all this
But first we'll watch Bake Off

If only Bake Off lasted six months
The nation would watch television

Three Things That Cheered Me Up
On A Wet Wednesday
#202 / 23:09:2020

Didn't watch the news
My new book arrived early
And Everton won

It Must Be Nearly Christmas
#203 / 24:09:2020

If that kipper tie still fitz
And you'd like a glam rock blitz
All the glitter, all the glitz
All the mis-spelt hits and bitz
Stomp those platform boots coz itz
Slade's new Cum On Feel The Hitz

The Forgotten
#204 / 25:09:2020

Purveyors of performing arts
Who strike the right notes, lift our hearts
All of those who tread the boards
Sing the songs and play the chords

All the actors and performers
All who entertain and warm us
Those who tour, those who've played
Every venue, every stage

Those who roll, those who rock
All those folk who've had to stop
Those who gigged most every night
And now they just can not

Those who took the centre stage
Those behind the scenes who've made
All the props and all the sets
Painted backdrops and effects

Costumiers, make-up appliers
Those who lug the amplifiers
Plug in plugs, re-wire wires
Backstage drinks and food suppliers

Those who drive the vans and who
Shout in mics – one-two, one-two
Those who tune and change the strings
A million other unseen things

Those who rap and those who rhyme
Dames dressed up in pantomime
Chorus singers, all the dancers
Extras waiting for their chances

Thespians and fools and clowns
Who nightly brought those curtains down
Musicians – every style, persuasion
Every genre and occasion

Those who rock and those who roll
Lift the spirits, feed the soul
Cherish theatre and live music
If we don't protect it then we lose it

Terms And Conditions
#205 / 26:09:2020

The precedent is evident
With numbers at their peak
Holed up in halls of residence
Their future looking bleak

Isolation – education
Pay your fees – don't speak
Money's earnt – lessons learnt
Brand new term – Freshers ... weak

Until Now
#206 / 27:09:2020

It's the quickest time ever
To fill a brand new notebook
With new poems, new ideas
Lists of things to do

But mostly new poems
Regular writing
Something I've always wanted
Something I've never had time for

Until now

Because You're Worth It?
#207 / 28:09:2020

Donald's done his taxes and the fact is they are true
Seventy grand a year and that's the best that you can do?
What should be your pride of place and your crowning glory
Lawdy! Darn it! With that barnet you're the clown in every story
With that coiffure not so sure you'd survive a windy day
Is that blond mop the best you've got – or just a higher price toupee?
You put the sty in style, it's also tax deductable
At seventy grand a year it should be indestructible
You don't need a barber, a stylist or beautician
With hair like that sir what you need is Merlin the Magician

Just Another Spoke In The Unreal
#208 / 29:09:2020

Confusing for everyday folk
It's getting beyond a bad joke
When our trusted PM
Has blundered again
This joke of a bloke who misspoke

Positive Signs?
#209 / 30:09:2020

Today's poem is short
I've got a school visit
A positive sign of better times?
… Or is it?

Seeing It Like A Poet On National Poetry Day
#210 / 01:10:2020
"Seeing it like a poet" was this year's theme.

I've been "seeing it like a poet"
For over thirty years now
Actually, not true
Much longer than that

Writing poems for most of my life
Publishing since eighteen
Job since 1989

Not so much
"Seeing like a poet" then
My life isn't a simile
It's a fact

Seeing it as a poet
Every single day
Where every day
Is a poetry day

The Day After National Poetry Day
Is Still National Poetry Day
#211 / 02:10:2020

It is the day after National Poetry Day
And it is still national poetry day
As it will be tomorrow
And the day after that
And the …

Remember
A poem is not just for
National Poetry Day
It's for life

Sympathy For The Devil
#212 / 03:10:2020

Positives are negatives – but we can make an exception
Positively negative – concerning the election
This presidential evidence … it may not be a coma
But Donald's been infected – I feel sorry for Corona

How this came to be may remain a mystery
But he's obviously more positive than anyone in history
More positively positive, the biggest virus owner
Donald's been infected – I feel sorry for Corona

Oh irony of ironies – this potential re-electant
And now it is the virus that is craving disinfectant
And bleach that will beseech, be a healer and atoner
Donald's been infected – I feel sorry for Corona

All that hate and bigotry and everything that's mean
Mutating with germs and strains in COVID-19
The outcome's looking ugly for the presidential moaner
Donald's been infected – I feel sorry for Corona

Pride that comes before a fall but not a fall from grace
For grace is not an issue – you were never in that place
Humility and dignity – for you, it's a misnomer
Donald's been infected – I feel sorry for Corona

Self-isolation – fourteen days – let's hope it's a beginning
With luck it could be longer – then everyone is winning
Now halt the Twitter feed from this serial mobile phoner
Donald's been infected – I feel sorry Corona

A nation's national health and security's been breached
Indestructible? Untouchable? This white whale has been beached
Repercussions rumble from New York to Arizona
Donald's been infected – I feel sorry for Corona

You Can Snitch On Your Neighbour …
#213 / 03:10:2020

If there's hot tubs and parties like Animal House
But not if there's guns and they're out shooting grouse

10,000
#214 / 04:10:2020

10,000's not a number to be proud of
10,000 is too many anywhere
10,000 is a number that should warn us
10,000 are the reasons to take care

10,000 are the reasons we should not be lazy
10,000 are the reasons for abiding by the rules
10,000 are the reasons for sticking to the guidelines
10,000 are the reasons to not behave like fools

10,000 are the lives that are affected
Plus the 10,000 thousand more
10,000 – the number that unites us
For what the future has in store

On The Same Page As A Certain Mister Matlock
#215 / 05:10:2020

First it was Slade, then it was Sweet
Then you and The Damned – 'Neat Neat Neat'
As past and present become complete
An ex-Sex Pistol re-tweeted my tweet

I quoted you – now it's you to repeat
The words I wrote about the elite
As punk rock and poetry meet
And an ex-Sex Pistol re-tweeted my tweet

Those in power turn up the heat
On artists as they try to compete
Live music – dead on its feet
And an ex-Sex Pistol re-tweeted my tweet

Never mind their b******s – their deceit
No surrender – no defeat
Long live the arts – our heartbeat
An ex-Sex Pistol re-tweeted my tweet

Just Not Enough
#216 / 06:10:2020

Technically speaking
We don't have children anymore
Twenty-seven and twenty
Adults

But you never stop being a parent
Ridiculously proud of their achievements
Worried by their decisions
Heartbroken at their mistakes

We may share the highs
But we also share the lows
Perhaps more so
Because we can see beyond 'the now'

Still our babies
We still want to protect them
Make the wrong things right
Take away their pain and hurt

But that is not our job anymore
Even if they let us
We may be parents
But we are powerless

And all we have is our love
And sometimes, sometimes
That love is not enough
Just not enough

Dear Mister Sunak – Hush Your Refrain
#217 / 07:10:2020

Just a thought that they ought shows total disdain
Oblivious, obviously – time and again
A lack of respect and concern that you feign
So hush your refrain that some should retrain

It isn't just stupid – but mad and insane
Ill-judged and ignorant, innately inane
As anyone knows who's got half a brain
So hush your refrain that some should retrain

So out of touch and yet still you claim
That you understand the stress and the strain
Your platitudes drip like rain down a drain
So hush your refrain that some should retrain

Just tell us again – just try to explain
The logic within – just what will it gain?
How can this help? Just what is your aim?
So hush your refrain that some should retrain

Art's at the heart of everything sane
So keep your mouth shut, let your head hang in shame
Hush your refrain that some should retrain
Perhaps all of you should do just the same

Living The Retraining Scheme Dream
#218 / 08:10:2020

Stormzy is serving in Subway
Adele's on the checkout at Asda
Ed Sheeran is now a lollipop man
Stopping the cars driving faster

Take That are delivery drivers
Dua Lipa is now a barista
Paloma Faith is now the new face
At Boots selling stuff to your sister

Jagger and Richards – a firm you can trust
For all your botanical needs
Jeff Lynne and Co – the new ELO
Electric Light Offers in Leeds

Ozzy is now in the priesthood
His confessions are better than yours
Macca's a driver for SAGA
Organising OAP tours

Harry has opened his new 'Hairy Styles'
Morrisey's serving in Greggs
Bono's now a beautician
Doing back, sack and crack with The Edge

The Arctic Monkey's deliver to Iceland
Tom Jones is at B&Q
So is Rod Stewart and Brian May
Cliff Richard is helping out too

Phil Collins is now a chauffeur here and there
His car – he'll expertly park it
Lewis Capaldi is managing Aldi
Sting's selling pants down the market

Little Mix now serve fish and chips
Not really got the X-Factor
Shirley Bassey is looking less classy
On her Massey Ferguson tractor

Boy George is building up burgers
On an M62 service station
Shane McGowan's a railway announcer
Messing up your destination

Olly Murs now works in healthcare
Clapton is now a mechanic
Elton has got his barbers
Now there's a reason to panic

The Gallagher brothers are plumbers
Do you really want them near your drain?
Rishi is singing the blues
It's what happens when we all retrain

Friday's Poem Is Often Short
Because It's The Day I Do My Weekly Shop
#219 / 09:10:2020

The crisis of COVID continues
The numbers they rise as we speak
But Boris won't panic about the pandemic
He'll make an announcement next week

Moving The Goalposts
#220 / 10:10:2020

I started off thinking "when"
Now it's more like "if"
More often than not these days ...
"Never"
And even though it's nothing to do with football
I long for the words of Kenneth Wolstenholme

They think it's all over ...
It is now

COVID that is
Not the world

Term Starts
#221 / 11:10:2020

Rainy Saturday
Heavy hearts
Daughter leaves
Term starts

Uncertain times
Distant parts
Isolation
Term starts

Numbers rise
COVID charts
Fear factor
Term starts

Coronavirus
Dark arts
Troubled waters
Term starts

Love is strong
Far apart
Daughter leaves
Term starts

Poem For A Monday
#222 / 12:10:2020

A poem for a Monday
Should try and give hope
At the beginning of a new week

A poem for a Monday
Should do something to allay
The so-called oft-quoted blues

A poem for a Monday
Should not be manic
But do something positive

So, today – this Monday
Phone your family
Tell them that you love them

Text a friend
With something uplifting
Smile at a stranger two metres away

And you can be the poem
The living poetry in motion
For a Monday

And every day

Today Demands A Poetic Response Much More Serious Than The One That Springs To Mind ...
#223 / 13:10:2020

We are told – we must be brave
As winter looms – looking grave
Everyone's a loser when it comes down to this lockdown

Puns and clichés sally forth
Ee bah gum – it's grim oop north
And all we seem to get are the Tiers of a Clown

The Jolly Man Who Doesn't Like Bad News
#224 / 13:10:2020

The bearer of bad tidings – not who he wants to be
The teller of home truths – it's not him, honestly
The facts he really wants to share – he'd like to pick and choose
He's the jolly man who doesn't like bad news

He'll talk around the houses – up the garden path
Will not give straight answers to the questions that we ask
Deflect it all with platitudes, disguised as heartfelt views
The jolly man who doesn't like bad news

He'll shy away from action – avoid all confrontation
Trying to appease and please – all bluff and hesitation
Harsh decision may cost votes he can't afford to lose
The jolly man who doesn't like bad news

No chance for jocularity or comments, off the cuff
Or endless popularity – we've all had enough
Just not what he really wants – when it comes to PMQs
The jolly man who doesn't like bad news

Clichéd and laborious – takes ages to say nothing
All a mask to cover up the fluster and the bluffing
Inaction and distraction, hints, half-truths and clues
The jolly man
The jolly man
This folly man without a plan
Who doesn't like bad news

I Just Don't Know What To Believe Anymore
But Some Of You Seem To Be Doing Okay
#225 / 14:10:2020

Perpetuated chaos and you have the temerity
To claim that you are acting with concern and with sincerity
Orchestrating ostracising regional austerity
When what we need the most is equality and clarity

What is fact or fiction – in this situation?
The fact is there are factions, division in the nation
And perpetuation, the fiscal segregation
Action is imperative and not deliberation

Messages are mixed and the science breeds confusion
Elasticated facts fabricating the delusion?
Suits and ties – truth or lies? Real or illusion?
The only thing that's certain is there is no solution

Those with conspiracies continue with their theorising
But nothing now is shocking and neither is it now surprising
The only constant seems to be the numbers and they keep on rising
Is it just our hands or the truth that we are sanitising?

Dear Diary
#226 / 15:10:2020

Samuel Pepys didn't make his rhyme
So why I am trying to do that with mine?

Anne hid hers from Nazi gun and tank
Mine – I'm just being honest and frank

Far too old to use the word "dork"
But I'll write what I want in the way that I talk

I may be wimpy – but no longer a kid
Cheap jokes and puns – to you, ten quid!

Adrian Mole was really a woman
If that's true here – who saw that comin'?

Is It Too Early For A Choccy Biscuit?
#227 / 16:10:2020

I've only just had breakfast and a second cup of tea
Wandered round the house a bit, sat on the settee
The tin is by the kettle – how can I resist it?
The only nagging question …
Is it still too early to have a choccy biscuit?

Answered all my messages – of which, there was one
Answered my work emails too – namely … none
What to do right now then – one option should I list it
Is that nagging question …
Is it still too early to have a choccy biscuit?

I could choose a healthy snack – from the fruit bowl, seldom touched
Try an apple every day … thank you very much
Start a carton of fresh juice – take the top and twist it
But still the nagging question …
Is it still too early to have a choccy biscuit?

Or make myself a smoothie – with strawberries and bananas
And run the risk of fruit stains down the front of my pyjamas
It may just be a chance that's slim but I'd rather that I missed it
And then there is the question …
Is it still too early to have a choccy biscuit?

Kettle on – resistance gone, I just couldn't hack it
A cup of tea is far too wet without at least a packet
Hobnob's choice, or something like that – oh go on I'll risk it
It isn't just a question
More of a suggestion
Sod the indigestion
It never is too early to have a choccy biscuit

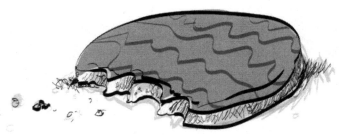

This Poem
#228 / 17:10:2020

This poem has no rhyme
Each line is different
Chaotic even

Sometimesit'sjustamassofwordsfightingforspaceandtobeheard

Then
It's
Isolated
   Words
                       And

                                        Sad phrases
This poem is
All
                                               Over
                      The

   Place

Not knowing what to do for the best

However, this poem is current
This poem is today

This poem has no rhyme or reason

Because this poem is current
This poem is today

Three Letters That Ruin Football
#229 / 18:10:2020

Very
Awkward
Replays

Vernacular
Added
Rhetoric

Variable
Angles
Reviewed

Voices
Are
Rising

Violent
Actions
Rejected

Vent
And
Rage

Vigorous
Application
Reneged

Vilified
And
Ridiculed

Verdict
Awful
Really

Vapid
Average
Referees

Vendetta
Against
Reality

Viable
Alternative
Required

Cuppa
#230 / 19:10:2020

"The first cup of tea in the morning is always the best"
Mum always says that
And she's right
"Sets you up for the day"

Milk, no sugar
Hope in a favourite mug
Doesn't really taste of anything
But still a proper brew

As a child
Before the advent of tea bags
Tea leaves were the stuff of nightmares
As they festooned and swirled
So I never drank right to the bottom of the cup
In case they invaded my infant mouth
Like tiny mutant tadpoles

A habit that continues today
As I drink most of it
Swill the rest away
Think of mum and dad
And what the day may bring

Eddie, Michael, Chuck, Ryan, Laura ...
And Now, Bruce – Six Of The Very Best
#231 / 20:10:2020
It's been an American sort of year – musically, not politically, obviously.

First, I fell in love with a girl called Eddie
All over again
Then Michael unlocked his soul
Chuck rocked, rolled and smiled in style

Ryan went away, came back with instant magic
Laura opened her broken beautiful heart
And Bruce did and does what Bruce does best
Especially with friends from E Street

Songs that reached out across the ocean
A universal language in melodies
A soundtrack to a lockdown time
Friends for life that lifted spirits

And touched my heart in the tenderest of ways
These are the songs that I shall return to
Again and again and again
These are the songs that will remain

A Girl Called Eddie – 'Been Around'
Michael McDermott – 'What in the World'
Chuck Prophet – 'The Land That Time Forgot'
Ryan Hamilton & The Harlequin Ghosts – 'Nowhere to Go But Everywhere'
Laura Veirs – 'My Echo'
Bruce Springsteen – 'Letter to You'

Is Manchester United?
#232 / 21:10:2020

Is Manchester united
Or a city now divided?
Has Boris got it right
Or made a call that's uninvited?

Is London now derided?
Is Manchester united?
Has Boris been short-sighted
And is it all one-sided?

Can any wrongs be righted
Or answers be provided?
Is Manchester united
And Blighty really blighted?

Brave or just strong minded?
Foolish or misguided?
Is Britain now divided
Or is Manchester united?

No Wonder
#233 / 22:10:2020

Free meals for children
Most affected by poverty and austerity

In a so-called caring society
Crisis after crisis, misery unprecedented

Answer me this …
Just what is there to vote against?

So this is what you've done
Just what have we become?

No wonder we heard the word "scum"

No Such Thing
#234 / 23:10:2020

There's no such thing as a free lunch
For a child in austerity

There's no such thing as a free lunch
Unless you're a working MP

The Never-Ending Same Old Story
#235 / 24:10:2020

Meet all needs – use all your powers
Judge not from those distant towers

Victims – young, of circumstance
A chance for your compassionate stance

A chance ignored to show you care
You're losing votes you borrowed there

See the funding – on a plate
Doled out to those who will donate

Contacts lead to new contracts
Snouts in troughs – them's the facts

It's the story that won't go away
Just like hunger faced each day

It's the story that rumbles on
Just like the stomachs of children wronged

Irony Is Always Lost On Those Who Will Not See
#236 / 25:10:2020

Twitter moral outrage as Conservatives close ranks
Reacting as they go on the defensive

"Picaninnies, letterboxes, watermelon smiles,
Bum boys" – apparently not offensive

All this moral high ground over etymology
Outrage for the blinkered and the angry

Outrage should be reserved for morality
Issues like children going hungry

Pronouncement
(In two haiku verses)
#237 / 26:10:2020

A vaccine pronounced
Which is more than you can say
About its makers

You say "Puh-fizer"
I say "Fizer" but let's not
Call the whole thing off

Twitter Feeds ...
#238 / 27:10:2020

Trial by Twitter
Trial by troll
Judge and jury
From those who cannot spell

Anger and spite
Bullying with cap-locks
Armchair experts
Laptop aggressors

Keyboard warriors
Invisible assassins
Everyone's an authority
Everyone's got a point to make

Online liars
Truth denouncers
Hate spreaders
Two hundred and eighty characters

Public and convenient
The world's biggest toilet wall
And if you read graffiti on toilet walls
There's always the stench of human waste

Soundbites
#239 / 28:10:2020

Holiday Hunger
Sounds almost friendly
Less serious, trivial

Holiday Hunger
Like waiting for candy floss
Or chips at the seaside

Holiday Hunger
Smiles and good times
A fun snack between meals

Holiday Hunger
Sugar-coated soundbite
Easier to swallow

For some

The Country Have Got Their Sports
Personality Of The Year Winner Right Now
#240 / 29:10:2020

Role model and superstar
On and off the pitch
Always in the spotlight
Can't switch off that switch

Hungry kids and hat-tricks
Always front page news
Tory Blues cannot defend
A match they're going to lose

Personality of the year
Sporting and a hero
Marcus – twenty million and three
Boris – big fat zero

Bobby ... Rock On
#241 / 30:10:2020
for Bobby Ball

Always something special, likeable
Actually, much more than that – loveable
We think of your mischievous glint
And cannot help but smile

Never hip, always funny
Always cheeky, never rude
A comedian tells jokes, a comic is funny
You were a comic – funny bones

More than expanding red braces
And a catchphrase
You took silliness seriously
Slapstick as art

No agenda, no axe to grind
No pretension, just warmth and connection
We felt you'd be our mate if we met you
And if we'd met you, you would have been just that

Laughter never dies
Everybody loves Bobby
Ball of fun
Total entertainment

Half of something special
A laugh track for our years
And we know with all our hearts
Your wishes and words would be

Rock on Tommy

Toothless – Not You
#242 / 31:10:2020
for Nobby Stiles

We all could be like you, sir – tenacious in the tackle
Get stuck in – you'd muck in, up for every battle
We dreamed of Best and Charlton but couldn't do what they could do
You gave us hope and glory … toothless – not you

You knew your place and reason – win it, give it, go
A man for every season – dogged little so and so
More than just enforcer, example through and through
Ruthless – yes of course, sir, but toothless – not you

A little bit of Nobby Stiles in everyone who's kicked a ball
The commitment to compete and always, always give your all
You made us feel that when we play we could do that too
The engine and the energy … toothless – not you

For club and then for country – the heart and soul of every team
For the people, of the people – you lived out our every dream
European Champion, a World Cup winner who
Was an ordinary hero … toothless – not you

A man we all relate to, we love and won't forget
Forever captured in that jig, you're still dancing yet
The chosen generation, one of the golden few
Honest, ever humble … toothless – not you

Legend, inspiration – the truth that's ever true
That grin we all remember, that win we all remember
Nobby Stiles, you made us smile
Toothless – not you

It's A Great Time To Be Royal Blue
#243 / 01:11:2020
A BBC commission for their coverage of the 2020 Women's FA Cup Final.

In the midst of a moment that's special
Built on the promise of more
On the shoulders of giant foundations
The legends who've led us before
Now is the time to look forward
An era that beckons anew
Stars aligned – in ascension
It's a great time to be royal blue

Trailblazing new inspirations
Role models for each boy and girl
Heroes for new generations
To go out and take on the world
Sharing the goals and the tackles
Joining with all that we do
Part of the family that battles
It's a great time to be royal blue

Unity in our community
A light in a time that is dark
This – our unique opportunity
To sprinkle some joy in each heart
Now is the time to dream all the dreams
For the many and not just the few
Playing with style – flying so high
It's a great time to be royal blue

Together, embracing this challenge
Together we're going to get through
Time to be great – as Wembley awaits
Chosen and royal and blue
In the midst of this moment that's special
Loyal – and royal – and true
History known – never alone
It's a great time to be royal blue

Just What Can We Say That Hasn't Been Said Before
#244 / 02:11:2020

Things have not got better, things haven't changed at all
Here we are again with our backs against the wall
Winter gloom of lockdown looms behind each closing door
Just what can we say that hasn't been said before?

Seven months of practise now, it's not a new surprise
Yet still we see incompetence, the failures and the lies
History repeating – we all know what's in store
Just what can we say that hasn't been said before?

COVID isn't over – as all the numbers rise
Those who will not hear and cover up their eyes
Those liars and deniers and fools who just ignore
Just what can we say that hasn't been said before?

All the dilly-dallying, all the hesitating
All the shilly-shallying, what's the point of waiting?
Learn from past mistakes and this time do much more
Just what can we say that hasn't been said before?

Direction and consistency, honesty and clarity
Compassion backed with actions, equality and parity
That is what we want, what we are asking for
Just what can we say that hasn't been said before?

"Perfect analysis ... Your poems have helped us all so much. You have
so often, and so skilfully, put my own thoughts into beautiful / angry /
amusing / heart-breaking verse." *Janet New*

An American Dream – Or Is It A Nightmare Scenario?
#245 / 03:11:2020

I have a dream
That you will open your eyes
See truth, see justice, see honesty
Look full in the face of opportunity
And do the right thing

I have a dream
That you will see hate for what it is
Reject those who perpetuate division
Those who would spread ignorance
Those whose lies have blighted you
Those who have held you back
And made you a laughing stock

It is time to put childish ways behind you
Time to choose wisdom
Not foolishness
And may all those fools who prosper
Fade away

May their mistakes be rectified
Their failings be recognised
May their sins be forgiven
May wounds be healed
And may you move onwards
Upwards
Forwards
Side by side

America, I have a dream
That you will do the right thing
For everyone

... That's Why I'm Sidin' With Biden

#246 / 04:11:2020

I don't really know – that much about Joe
And the answers he may be providin'
But mainly the fact – he's not Donald Trump
That's why I'm sidin' with Biden

It's not cut and dried – they've yet to decide
What's best for a country that's slidin'
But mainly the fact that he's not Donald Trump
That's why I'm sidin' with Biden

We'll all have to wait – for who makes it great
As the blue and the red are collidin'
But mainly the fact he's not Donald Trump
That's why I'm sidin' with Biden

The hate and the spite, his lean to the right
The secrets and lies that he's hidin'
And still the people are votin' for Trump
That's why I'm sidin' with Biden

There's no discountin' the pressure that's mountin'
The surge of the surf that he's ridin'
But all of these motorcade haters for Trump ...
That's why I'm sidin' with Biden

It's goin' to be close – much closer than most
The smallest of margins decidin'
But mainly the fact he's not Donald Trump
That's why I'm sidin' with Biden

The alternative's worse – a national curse
Disaster that's worse than Poseidon
You reap what you sow with the Trump you all know
That's why I'm sidin' with Biden

So much is clear from company kept ...
Nigel Farage and John Lydon
Ignorant, bonkers, irrelevant
That's why I'm siding' with Biden

Fireworks Expected
#247 / 05:11:2020

Remember, remember
The vote in November
Conspiracy theory and plot
The pressure is mounting
As they keep on counting
Trump thinks he's won but he's not

Just What Is It About Donald?
#248 / 06:11:2020

Maybe you're not the monster
Maybe you're not the joke
Maybe there's something different
That made so many vote

Bleach and radiation
And still they all believe you
Seeming random madness
And still they would receive you

You must have something different
That some have never seen
Just what is the real appeal
Of your American Dream?

You never played the politics game
The one who bucked the system
An outsider who came inside
And never became distant

Direct and to the point
Eminently tweet-able
Are you the people's champion?
Accessible and reachable

An honesty in crassness
Perhaps that's the attraction?
Say it like you think it is
Affrontery and action

An army of supporters
Exactly what you've got
You speak their language
Whether you mean it or not

Our a-biden memory
No ordinary Joe
You asked America a question
They didn't all say no

It Don't Mean A Thing If That State's Got A Swing
#249 / 07:11:2020

Donald – there in Georgia, he
Claims electoral forgery

Things are getting horrider
Even though he leads in Florida

It's suddenly much harder
With nada in Nevada

A whinger and a moaner
About the votes in Arizona

But strangely is no whiner
When it comes to Carolina

Donald ducks the questions
In the saloon of this last chancer

Quack quack quack quack cracking up
Donald Duck's the answer

Lest We Now Forget
#250 / 08:11:2020

Bravery and bloodshed
None can comprehend
Passing time, it heals not
Nor the sorrow mend
Heroes who have fallen
So long ago and yet
Flowers of remembrance
Lest we now forget

This then, is our tribute
All that we can give
For those sacrifices
So that we may live
Names and unknown soldiers
Those we never met
Flowers of remembrance
Lest we now forget

Let us now remember
Those who've gone before
And we pray that peace may
Conquer every war
May we tread no longer
Pathways of regret
Flowers of remembrance
Lest we now forget

History, though distant
Bids us all recall
With our hearts and souls now
We salute you all
Silent contemplation
Join and pay respect
Flowers of remembrance
Lest we now forget

Sweet F.A.
#251 / 09:11:2020

Rashford 2 – Johnson 0
That's what the scoreboards say
But it shouldn't take a footballer
To lead the way today

Own goals scored – yet again
The usual state of play
But it shouldn't take a footballer
To lead the way today

Extra time was needed
And that is not okay
It should not take a footballer
To lead the way today

If a footballer can see what's right
And wrong and you can not
Just how can we trust you?
What chance have we got?

"When looking at the national landscape, its wounds and doughty perseverance generated by its grief-besieged citizens, Paul Cookson is their sparse voice, their collective bewilderment and courage."
Stewart Henderson

Life's Too Short For Burnt Toast
#252 / 10:11:2020

Making breakfast
And thinking about today's poem
I was distracted
And left the toaster on too long

Being of a certain age
And averse to waste
I buttered the blackened bread
And took a bite

Just one
Then threw it away
And started again
With more care and precision

Life's too short for burnt toast
Things are depressing enough
You've got to make the most of the little things
Like tea and toast

And poetry

The Last Post
#253 / 11:11:2020

This poem was inspired by a tweet from Badly Drawn Boy:
"My Dad was 2 or 3 when his Father was killed in WW2. They recovered his wallet with a letter which had a hole through it. He'd been stabbed with a bayonet. The letter said 'How's little Rick? [my Dad] I can't remember what he looks like.'."

A letter from the trenches
From a man I never met
A letter never sent
And a German bayonet

There's a hole inside my heart
As I think about it yet
The letter pierced and torn
By a German bayonet

Those written words live on
Lest ever we forget
A letter stained with horror
From a German bayonet

Forever left its mark
Such sorrow and regret
A letter from my Grandfather
And a German bayonet

They're Giving Us Hope To Distract Us
#254 / 12:11:2020

A reason to be cheerful
A cause for optimism
Vaccine for a nation
A Christmas-time decision

A tunnel that seemed endless
Dark and black as night
Is suddenly a tunnel
Where there's now a chink of light

But look behind the headlines
Where money has been spent
Who has benefitted most
And it's evident

That everything's not crystal clear
And far from as it seems
As we are all distracted by
Vaccination dreams

Incestuously connected?
Or just coincidental?
As Holmes would say to Watson
"Simply elemental"

Try as you might, it doesn't add up
Whatever the calculation
They're hoping to distract us
With a Christmas vaccination

As The Old Song Says ...
#255 / 13:11:2020

There's tantrums in The White House
From the one who's playing kings
Toys are out the pram
And littering the wings
Screaming and a-shouting
He can't pull any strings
He won't budge a single inch
By fingernails he clings
Covering both ears up
Won't listen to a thing
Spitting out his dummy
One last crazy fling
Playing tweety tweety games
Another caps locks pings
So I guess it isn't over
'Til the fat baby sings

As A Rat Leaves Let's Hope The Whole Ship Sinks
As You Walk Away With A Cardboard Box
Like A Minor Character In An American B-Movie
#256 / 14:11:2020

Vermin unbecoming
At long, long last you're goin'
Not even worth another line
In a stupid poem

Windmills

#257 / 15:11:2020

Not a new poem, in fact probably my very first ever poem, aged 10 in Mrs Burton's Class, Little Hoole County Primary School. First published poem certainly, as it was in her school anthology. I didn't know of its existence until Joan (Mrs B) sent me this via Facebook. No changes have been made since 1971.

One day I saw a windmill there
In a field of tulips fair
The tulips they belong to farms
And the windmills all have swinging arms

In a field – bright and gay
One windmill seemed to say
"How I wish the wind would stop
My sails are spinning like a top"

The sails are spinning in the breeze
The miller grinds the corn with ease
Sometimes fast and sometimes slow
That's the way the windmills go!

The sails go merrily whirling round
Sometimes nearly touching the ground
All of them belong to farms
Those windmills with their swinging arms

"Your skill with words is amazing and your discipline is second to none. I'm so proud of you." *Joan Burton*

A Little Less Sunshine
#258 / 16:11:2020
for Des O'Connor

Your name
Once synonymous with rubbish
Thanks to your biggest fans
Des ... short for Desperate

You embraced it all
Became part of the joke
Laughed it all up
Consummate professional

In an age where "light entertainment"
Has become cliché, parody
Or even an insult
You had it all

A song, a dance, a joke, a smile
It wasn't just star quality
That drew the audience in
It was warmth

That and lack of ego
Made us love you all the more
As for over fifty years
You only brought us sunshine

Ungloved But Never Unloved
#259 / 17:11:2020
for Ray Clemence

It didn't matter who you supported
You were one of the good guys
Always

In an era where footballers
Looked like a mate of your uncle
You were everything and ordinary

Agility and bravery
Guardian of Liverpool and England
Unassuming force to be reckoned with

All were in safe hands
We trusted you
On and off the pitch

Gentleman ambassador
Everyday enthusiast
Ultimate professional

Keeper without fear
Goalie without gloves
The man between the sticks
That everybody loves

Ten Billion Pounds Of Flesh
#260 / 18:11:2020

So very, very, very proud
Of all our work with PPE
Plus, lots of friends are richer too
That's how it all should be

Heard Immunity
#261 / 19:11:2020

There may be talk of vaccines
Somewhere on the horizon
But the figures do not lie
As the dying keep on rising

Numbed by all the numbers
Confused by all the views
We've developed heard immunity
To politics and news

Donald's Discount Offers Failing
#262 / 20:11:2020

Without any shadow of doubt
The pressure's beginning to mount
No turn that's spectacular
The truth is like Dracula
There's just no stopping the count

Where There's A Bully There's Always A Bull
And Where There's A Bull There's Always Bullst**
#263 / 21:11:2020

You can't do a job very well
If you have to shout, swear and yell
To understand fully
Just what is a bully …
It's not looking pretty, Patel

The Boy Who Saved Christmas
#264 / 22:11:2020

'Twas the month before Christmas when all through the land
Families are worried about what they have planned
Things are rock bottom with COVID-19
Annus horribilis – just like the Queen

We all want a tree, bright lights and holly
'Tis not the season for us to be jolly
Christmas is cancelled, that's how it appears
Instead of the baubles, there's bubbles and tiers

Self-isolation and turkey for one
Lonely this Christmas is not that much fun
But one little chappy has made it his mission
To make things alright with his big decision

Let's all get together, let's all relax
Forget all the science, forget all the facts
Let's all have a good time, a party December
A blow out, let's go out but let's all remember

It won't all be good news, fun and good cheer
We'll have to stay in when it comes to new year
While the promise of vaccines arrive thick and fast
Our plucky young hero has made it his task

To rescue the season from lockdown and misery
So he'll be remembered and go down in history
As the boy who saved Christmas, brought families together
And the name of young Boris shall live on forever!

Not Confused At All
#265 / 23:11:2020

Hoorah – the good news is this
We can celebrate amidst all this mess
Consider this and please don't dismiss
A three-family five-day Christmas

On The Day That The News Is All About Vaccine –
That's The Day I Feel Ill
#266 / 24:11:2020

Today's poem has been cancelled
Without too much warning
Normal service
Resumed in the morning

If Only The Foo Fighters Had A Really Famous Song
That I Could Use As A Pun For The Flu Fighters ...
Nevermind
#267 / 25:11:2020
A short poem with historical rock and roll puns.

A day in bed
Aching head
Aching back and aching legs

At least it's not The Knack and 'My Corona'
More Johnny Kidd and 'Aching All Over'

Little Genius, Flawed And Human
#268 / 26:11:2020
for Maradona

Men are defined by moments
Not careers – over years
But isolated flashes of skill, audacity
Those half-chance actions
That spontaneity and artistry that captures the imagination

You could have been defined by skill sublime
Fleet of foot, a master craftsman
An artist at work carving through the resistance
Sculpting your masterpiece with intricacy, delicacy
Effortless ease and exquisite talent
Your goal like a diamond, individual, precious and special

All true

This could have been your moment
Your defining slice of football history
The memory that elicits warmth and generosity of spirit
Respect, awe and credibility
Had you not already been defined forever
By the incredulity and crassness of an earlier action

Nothing to do with skill
But everything to do with audacity
And nothing to do with the beauty of the game

The fact you christened it your Hand of God
Just makes it worse
That and the fact you scored such a magical goal in the same match
A thing of pure beauty and spectacle

Genius – without a doubt
Flawed – without a doubt
Human – and that's why part us wanted to be like you

Short And To The Point
#269 / 27:11:2020

Back in bed
Extra rest
Booked a drive-through COVID test
Hope the answer isn't yes

Limersick
#270 / 28:11:2020

For five days and nights have I ailed
My temperature's risen and sailed
Changing and shaking
But good news that's breaking
The test that I took I have failed

Planning Ahead For Various Eventualities
#271 / 29:11:2020

I've been getting ahead of the game
While I have time and silence
This could be tomorrow's poem
Written in advance

Though, should something important
Thrust itself into the limelight
And therefore prove inspirational
This poem may have to wait

In which case, it will be stockpiled
Or if I'm too under the weather for a new one
In true Blue Peter fashion
It can be produced with the line

"Here's one I prepared earlier"

It's Always Good To Have A Different Approach
#272 / 30:11:2020

For nine months now
Every day has brought forth a new poem
Each one different to the last
Lines that map my poetic diary

Largely responding to the news
Inspired by my own situation, perhaps
Knowing that one day I can look back and
Experience the truth of these days

Striving to be original on a daily basis
Has occasionally felt like Mastermind
I've started – so I'll finish
Today, however, is my first deliberate acrostic

All This Time And Still ...
#273 / 01:12:2020

You'd have thought
That with over a week in bed
Staring at the ceiling
I would have had time
To think of lots of things to write about
Or plan lots of things that I should do
Once I get better
Books to read
Movies to catch up on
Mini-series to binge on

That's the trouble
I'm just
Listless

Numbers Don't Name Names
#274 / 02:12:2020

Numbers don't name names
Statistics are not personal
Another six hundred and three died
But only one I know by name

More than a Facebook friend
All round wonderful man
Taken
Just taken

We can talk about your open heart
Generosity of spirit
Shared interests and rock and roll passions
And the solidarity of friends and family

But the reality is the reality
Heart-breaking and brutal
And a vaccine around the corner
Is a corner too far

Numbers don't name names
And one day, maybe I'll have to delete
Both from the contacts of my phone
But not today, not today Dave

Fly The Flags, Play The Fanfares,
Hurrah And Huzzah
And Isn't Britain Great Again
#275 / 03:12:2020

Forget about our failures
At last we've passed a test
The first to get the vaccine
Because we are the best

On The Up
#276 / 04:12:2020

Although the bed has not been made
In two weeks now
Today was a step in the right direction
A day for underpants and deodorant

I must be feeling better
I applied both correctly

Lukewarm Ribena
#277 / 05:12:2020

For the first time in over a week now
I am sat upright at the table
And writing by the dining room window
Outside, snow and sleet swirls
Not enough snow to settle
But too much snow to be just rain
Inside, I am glad of central heating
And a lukewarm Ribena
That reminds me of childhood days like this

Ribena or Vimto always had
The ability to be diluted sufficiently
To outlast four children
A precursor to the cure-all
That was hot sugared tea
And a digestive biscuit
Actually, I have unwittingly lied
In that in the time it has taken to write this poem
The snow is now heavy enough to settle

And a second glass of lukewarm
Non-alcoholic claret warmth beckons
As does a return to bed
Today will not be a day for getting dressed

The Voice Of Golf

#278 / 06:12:2020
for Peter Alliss

Golf was never my sport of choice
But dad played so I'd borrow his old clubs
For pitch and putt and the like
In the back garden

Plus, he'd watch it on the telly
And, being a child who liked watching telly
I watched whatever dad was watching
Them's were the rules

So I watched golf
Checked trousers and diamond sweaters
Whether Grandstand or Sportsnight with Coleman
Or the pro-celebrity with Brucie, Tarby and Ronnie

But I also listened
To the voice of golf
Almost the voice of God
Peter Alliss

A voice not just associated with the sport
But with warmth, humour and self-deprecation
A voice that captures each moment perfectly
A voice that always makes us smile

Anyone who has ever swung a golf club
Whether back garden, park, pitch and putt or course
Has heard internally that commentary
And it has only ever been one voice

A commentator's commentator
That voice we have all grown up with
Mister Golf himself
Thank you, Peter Alliss

Clichés, Lies, Stupidity And Incompetence –
The Four Horsemen Of The Brexit Apocalypse
#279 / 07:12:2020

Like the lies upon the buses
And soundbites by the dozen

We haven't got a deal
Not even got an oven

Ready as we've never been
After all these years

Just like everything else
It all ends in tears

What A Nelly!
#280 / 07:12:2020

Donald the President won't pack his trunk
And say goodbye to his circus
He won't go with a trumpety-trump
Trump! Trump! Trump!

Donald the President won't pack his trunk
And head off back to the jungle
All alone with his mobile phone
Tweet! Tweet! Tweet!

It'sssss Veeeee Dayyyyyyy!

#281 / 08:12:2020

New words for a possibly recognisable tune.

Are you hanging all your hopes upon it all?
Are you hoping that the doctor's gonna call?
Never mind the pain dear – the Pfizer's on its way
So now it's safe to mix on Christmas Day ...

So here it is Merry Christmas
Everything will be okay
Look to the future now
It's Vaccination Day – ay – ay – ay

Are you waiting for the vaccine to arrive?
Have your fridges got the room to spare inside?
Does the PM always tell you that Great Britain is the best
And he's up and rock and rolling out the test ...

So here it is Merry Christmas
Everything will be okay
Look to the future now
It's Vaccination Day – ay – ay – ay

IT'SSSSS VEEEEE DAYYYYYYY!

The Ballad Of Battleground Brexit
#282 / 09:12:2020

Way, way back in 'sixteen
It was difficult to see who
Was going on and on and on
For us to leave the EU
No mass demonstrations
No furrowed fervour clammerin'
The battleground that Brexit brought
I blame David Cameron

No constant burning issue
That plagued and raged the nation
More, a few, small minded, who
Had mild consternation
No permanent petitions
Persistently a-hammering
Now – national dis-unity
I blame David Cameron

It almost seemed an idle whim
To have a national ballot
A complex nut like this to crack
Doesn't need a great big mallet
Yes or No – is not enough
This woolly vague flim-flammerin'
No detail in the details
I blame David Cameron

Gove, Farage and Johnson
The blind who led the bland
The lies upon the buses
That travelled 'cross this land
Hoodwinked and mugged by chancers
And their jingoistic yammerin'
Rule Britannia and the rest ...
I blame David Cameron

Democracy it isn't
When based upon deception
Ignorance is voter's bliss
When you lead an insurrection
Let's all guard our little home
"Don't panic Mister Mainwaring"
Dad's Army, Queen and country ...
I blame David Cameron

A nation split and shattered
Thanks to that referendum
Picking up the pieces while
We want a happy ending
Let's hire a fleet of double-deckers
Each with a massive banner on

PIG'S EAR AND DOG'S DINNER
THANK YOU MISTER CAMERON

Sovereignty, Our Sovereignty
#283 / 10:12:2020

Sovereignty – ah sovereignty
At least we have our sovereignty
A triumph of democracy
Sovereignty, our sovereignty

The prize we sought defiantly
The battle won so valiantly
Worth the wait so patiently
Sovereignty, our sovereignty

A Brexit handled brilliantly
An outcome planned so carefully
Where we agree to disagree
Sovereignty, our sovereignty

Protection of identity
Our right to nationality
Independent entity
Sovereignty, our sovereignty

Jam and scones and cream for tea
This sceptred isle, the place to be
No longer slaves, at last we're free
Sovereignty, our sovereignty

We'll fly our flag for all to see
God Save The Queen and dear country
In isolated mystery
Sovereignty, our sovereignty

Never mind economy
Jobs for you and jobs for me
Or prices rising dangerously
Sovereignty, our sovereignty

Years wasted needlessly
Hands held high so emptily
Negotiated fruitlessly
Sovereignty, our sovereignty

Nothing else for us to see
Like an empty Christmas tree
All is green and pleasantry
Sovereignty, our sovereignty

A notion based on history
We are more than geography
Nothing else to show but we
All have got our sovereignty

An Englishman's Comb Is His Hassle

#284 / 11:12:2020

With apologies to whoever I have borrowed this pun from – a Denis Norden book and a Nick Toczek poem.

The state of the nation is one situation
We shouldn't be willing to rush
But something more pressing is really distressing
Let's buy Boris a brush

It's wild and it's woolly, which sums him up fully
And won't stay in place with a push
Divided – whatever, let's all pull together
And buy poor Boris a brush

A life of its own, it seems to have grown
Like a mutating alien bush
Unkempt and uncared for, unstatesman-like therefore
Let's buy Boris a brush

Unlike the election, there's every direction
That's causing his centre to blush
It's left and it's right – like a fright in the night
Let's buy Boris a brush

Monstrous and raving, loony behaving
Worse than Screaming Lord Sutch
Looks like the child catcher, he now needs a thatcher
Let's buy Boris a brush

Entirely fitting, he could have been sitting
Near a lavat'ry waiting to flush
Like one for the toilet, don't spoil it or soil it
Let's buy Boris a brush

Hair gel or Brylcreem mixed up with Vaseline
Won't tame this mane very much
Won't keep it in place, a state of disgrace
Let's buy Boris a brush

In Other Words ...
#285 / 12:12:2020

A brand new day
A new cliché
A trade deal like Australia
Just a way
Not to say
How things have been a failure

Catchphrase – Say What You See
#286 / 13:12:2020
All phrases have been used – apart from one.

Go the extra mile
Walking over broken glass
Into extra time
One last push

Still got legs
Down to the wire
Out of the frying pan
Into the fire

Prepare Ye The Way
#287 / 14:12:2020

Like training for a marathon with a wander in your slippers
Fighting Tyson Fury in your Union Jack knickers

Going for Olympic gold with a diet based on pies
Playing Truth or Dare with a habit based on lies

Be a World Cup Winning Manager because you once played FIFA
Pretending to be Jesus because you like eggs at Easter

Publishing a novel 'cos the title's rather spiffing
The pages are all blank and the detail has gone missing

A Eurovision entry when you've got half a verse
West End centre stage without having to rehearse

You've only got a wooden spoon yet think you are Nigella
Stirring up big issues when you are just the programme seller

Trying to win on Strictly 'cause you once danced to the conga
Drunk and at the back of the line that's getting longer

You think you're indestructible – just like Captain Scarlett
A knight without a sword shouting "Have at thee, you varlet!"

Cramming for exams with last minute skim reading
In the knowledge that you've got a job thanks to genes and breeding

Front page news when there isn't any story
Minimum effort – maximum glory

Shouting slogans to a crowd trying to be heard
All this bloody time and still you're unprepared

Turning every drama into a downright farce
The higher that a monkey climbs, the more it shows its arse

'Tis The Season To Be Folly
#288 / 15:12:2020

We may have got a new vaccine
But that doesn't really mean
That everything's okay and the numbers keep on dropping
We may not all be liking
Those numbers that keep spiking
But nothing can be stopping the people Christmas shopping

Crowded streets are buzzing
Ten times to the dozen
It may not be a party with the party poppers popping
But the masses that are heaving
Unmasked and close and breathing
'Cause nothing can be stopping the people Christmas shopping

Oh 'tis the festive season
And selfishness, the reason
That caution's to the wind just to fill a Christmas stocking
Ignorance, stupidity
Irresponsibility
'Cause no-one can be stopping
These actions that are shocking
More trouble we're unlocking
Now lockdown seems forgotten
Nothing can be stopping the good people Christmas shopping

COVID Waits
#289 / 16:12:2020

COVID waits
Hibernates
Re-creates
Then mutates

Duplicates
Contaminates
Deviates
Then activates

Aggravates
Demonstrates
Deteriorates
Dominates

Rising rates
That translates
As dire straits
COVID waits

Goodwill To All
#290 / 17:12:2020

Christmas wishes, hugs and kisses
'Tis the season of good cheer
Love and joy, peace, goodwill
Let's hope that's all we spread this year

Shameful And Shameless
#291 / 18:12:2020

"UNICEF should be ashamed of itself." — *Jacob Rees-Mogg*

Look in the mirror, hear your own words
Privileged millionaire – on a limb and out of touch
And still you will not feel ashamed

I am ashamed
When I hear your words
Echoing like scattergun buckshot

Ashamed that you call yourself Christian
Yet display nothing of Christ
No compassion, no love, no empathy

Ashamed to live in a society
Where hunger is avoidable
But isn't – because of your policies

Shut your poisoned mouth
You are the one who should be ashamed
But that is not your way

Arrogance will see you through
And when you say your prayers at night
Just who do you pray to?

Let's Hope A Liddle Can Go A Long Way Away
#292 / 19:12:2020

"COVID has made heroes of many of our frontline workers... but not teachers."
— *Rod Liddle*

Vilified in headlines
By those who've never ever taught

Devalued in the public eye
By those who know no better

Criticised in print
Bitter lies and poison

Everyone's an expert
Just because they went to school

Ignorance outweighed
By monumental arrogance

Teachers teach and so much more
A job that never ever ends

Compassion, care, commitment
Oh – and the lessons too

Always above, always beyond
Never just the minimum

Frontline, firing line
Every single day

Teachers are not heroes?
You haven't got a clue

Priorities
#293 / 20:12:2020

There may be dark, dark days
Trouble ahead
But right now
I've got bigger problems ...
I can't find the end of the sodding Sellotape

True, there's isolation
Not being able to see the family
But that's not the issue here ...
I should have tried the outside lights first
Before spending two hours putting them up

Stuck in Tier Four
Whatever the hell that means these days
Who knows anymore?
But at the moment, it pales beside the fact
I'm still waiting for at least three parcels to arrive

The news goes on and on
About new strains of virus
The need to be vigilant
New spikes and more lockdown
But I can't think of that right now
When I've got to get down to the supermarket

Can't we just forget about COVID
For a few days?
Coronavirus doesn't really seem right
When it's the festive season
I mean, it is Christmas after all
And you have to get priorities right

Distant – Not Social
#294 / 21:12:2020

It's getting near that time
When most of the shopping has been done
Presents wrapped
Fridge and freezer stocked
And only a few last-minute tasks to do

That time when normally
Thoughts turn to packing an overnight bag
Planning journeys
Sorting travel arrangements
That extra bunch of flowers
A bottle of something nice
Maybe a casserole or pudding ... or both

But not this year
No travel plans to criss-cross the country
Or getting up early to miss the traffic
No braving the elements
Just to share the festive spirit

This year, we will sit at our own tables
With empty chairs and unused crackers
Phone or Zoom or FaceTime
And raise a glass to
Absent family and distant friends
Promising that we'll make up for it next year
When all this is over and we are back to normal

Déjà Vu ... Again
#295 / 22:12:2020

New news
New strain
New panic
New pain

Nothing learnt
Now we wait
Too little
Too late

Time for anger
Time for fears
Time for sadness
Time for tears

The Lies That You (Pa)tel
#296 / 23:12:2020

Of all the gall and the nerve
To say you're "ahead of the curve"
Your view and perspective
Is skewed and selective
Depends on which way you swerve

"A great commentary of these unusual and frightening times.
Just wish the Prime Minister had been reading with us.
Keep them coming please." *Jamie Bannister*

While Drivers Stopped
#297 / 24:12:2020

While drivers stop their trucks at night
All halted on the ground
Four thousand engines all switched off
And no-one made a sound

"Fear not" said he, at Number Ten
I'm sure we'll muddle through
Glad tidings of great joy I bring
Goodbye to the EU

All you parked on the motorway
So perfectly in line
May not move for many a day
Just waiting for a sign

I don't know what the sign will be
I haven't got a clue
I know it's not four thousand trucks ...
Hundred and seventy-two *

A sign of what the future holds
No sovereignty or peace
A sign of chaos yet to come
Begin and never cease

* *I know it's 170, but that didn't rhyme.*

Ode To The Last Sprout
#298 / 25:12:2020

There'll never be a tussle
For that final Brussel
No hassle and no hustle
No extra show of muscle

Nowt to fight about
For one last Brussel sprout
No need to scream and shout
Of that there is no doubt

A huff and puff and fuss'll
Ensue for the last truffle
But for the lonely Brussel
No scuffle or kerfuffle

All The Right Words
#299 / 26:12:2020

Whatever the year
Christmas isn't Christmas
Without Eric and Ernie

Like funny uncles
Always part of our family
We'd laugh together – really laugh

As someone once said
"It's not the jokes – it's the blokes"
What jokes, what blokes

Universal catchphrases
"You can't see the join", "Short fat hairy legs"
"He's not going to sell much ice cream going at that speed"

"What do you think of it so far?"
"Mister Preview" and everybody's cough
Was followed by the shout of "Arsenal!"

All became part of our family lexicon
Shared vocabulary
A knowing smile and wink

And so, I sit and watch again
Knowing all the looks
Word perfect with the lines

And think of dad
How he'd laugh
And how we'd watch and laugh together

Also, how I really wish
That at his funeral
When the service sheet was printed incorrectly

I'd said
"This sheet has all the right words
But not necessarily in the right order"

Everything Except ...
#300 / 27:12:2020

We've had turkey and cranberry
Chestnuts and carrots
Parsnips and sprouts – just as you would
Roasted potatoes – pigs in their blankets
But we haven't had a hug

There's been fancies and biscuits
Mince pies and stollen
Sauce made from brandy on Christmas pud
Fruit cake and icing – a million chocolates
But there hasn't been a hug

We've got tree decorations
Crackers and candles
Cards with a message for times that are good
Wishes with kisses
But everyone misses
The chance for a family hug

Daze
#301 / 28:12:2020

I'm not really sure what day it is
Feels like Sunday
But it's not
Yesterday didn't feel like a Sunday
But it was
Today doesn't feel like a Monday
But it is
That sort of forever time
Between Christmas and New Year
Where all the days melt into one
And every day just feels the same
With turkey being part of every meal
Along with the spare mince pies
And part of you just wants egg and chips

An Immaculate Deception
#302 / 29:12:2020

I have re-read the Christmas story
And to be honest, the notion of
A virgin birth, immaculate conception
Choirs of angels, wise men and stars
Is easier to understand
Than a No Deal Brexit
And current lockdown restrictions

Plus it makes more sense

Merry Christmas And A Happy New Fear
#303 / 30:12:2020

Distracted by the season
A tiny bit of cheer
Now comes the news
That no-one wants to hear

Infection numbers rising
One thing, crystal clear
Twenty twenty-one
No happy new year

Pick a number, any number
Add it to a tier
Another lockdown looming
Another year of fear

Bin There – Done That
#304 / 31:12:2020

It's that time of the year
When middle-aged overweight dads
Are glad of the extra Christmas pounds
As they navigate a garden chair
Use the garage wall or garden fence for guidance
Clumsily clamber into the blue bin
Jump up and down as many times
As energy and balance will allow
To squash the recycling down
Because the bin men aren't here 'til next week
But no-one really knows what day
So we all look at everyone else's drive
And hope we don't have to repeat the
Blue bin bad dad dance

Two Sides Of The Same Coin?
#305 / 01:01:2021

HEADS ...

May the year that lies before us
Be much better than the last

May the future yet unwritten
Be much better than the past

May the time unspent with loved ones
Simply fade away

May the company we keep
Bless us every day

May trials, tribulations
Be few or disappear

May the touch of friends and family
Embrace us through the year

OR TAILS ...

The first poem of the new year
Should be full of hope
Resolutions, new beginnings
Positivity and looking forward

But somehow, this year
It isn't ... yet

"A poignant and definitive record of a challenging, turbulent year."
Badly Drawn Boy

All
#306 / 02:01:2021

All you COVID non-believers
Truth deniers and deceivers
Doing just as you pleasers
Selfish to the last

All you so-called free thinkers
Fact ignorers, truth-tinkers
Just remove those narrow blinkers
Is that too much to ask?

All you who just want to see
Theories of conspiracy
With no responsibility
Playing loose and fast

All you fools with no compliance
Facebook posts your sole reliance
Know much more than all the science
Just don't make me laugh

All you keyboard ranting hacks
Experts who don't follow facts
Shouting loudest from the back
False news that you pass

All you selfish rule breakers
Frauds and fools and risk takers
Half-baked theory maker fakers
Time to face the facts

If not for you, then for others
Or respect for one another
It might help someone to recover
Just wear a bloody mask!

Once A Year I'm A Serial Killer
#307 / 03:01:2021

Yesterday was a day for
Seemingly mindless violence
The strangling of tangling cords
Pulled tighter and tighter with anger
The sawing of random limbs
Stuffed into a wheelie bin
Still ... that's the Christmas lights
And tree sorted for another year

More Than One Song –
But The Song Says Everything
#308 / 04:01:2021
for Gerry Marsden

Associated forever with football
But some things transcend rivalries
You may not have written it
But you made it your own
Universal love and recognition
So too, the tribute to your home
A legacy of music
Timeless and eternal
Gerry Marsden
Forever loved

I'm No Nostradamus But ...
#309 / 05:01:2021

Oh what a shock! A bolt from the blue!
Completely surprised ... Really? Who knew?

Who saw this coming? When did this appear?
Just who could predict Groundhog Year?

The King Who Never Wore A Crown
#310 / 06:01:2021
for Colin Bell

No matter our allegiances
Every football fan would tell
A favourite who we'd want to be
The one and only Colin Bell

Your feet just did the talking
True class, true great, less feted
Not rock star like the others
Humble, modest, understated

The king who never wore a crown
Never understood your fame
Club and country gentleman
Quiet man who ruled the game

And we all knew your name

Democracy Attacked
#311 / 07:01:2021

A process that is cracked
Unlawfully hijacked
Where idiots can act
Democracy attacked

A siege and that's a fact
Designed to counteract
Distort, destroy, distract
Democracy attacked

A despot blindly backed
A devil and a pact
Rioters react
Democracy attacked

Justice has been hacked
Everything is cracked
Trump to be exact
Democracy attacked

Two Words
#312 / 08:01:2021

Take your callous smiling face
Just go
Take your lack of love and grace
Just go
Take your chaos and confusion
Take your self-obsessed delusion
Take your tin pot revolution
Go
You've had your allotted time
And now the answer's "No"
Please Mister President
Just go

Take your bigotry and views
Just go
Take your ignorance and fake news
Just go
Take your idiot Twitter feed
Take your narcissistic greed
All the shit that we don't need
Go
Disappear to who cares where
No-one needs to know
Please Mister President
Just go

Take your reptilian grin of lies
Just go
The division in your ice-cold eyes
Just go
Take your false humility
Take your insincerity
Your intense stupidity
Go
Far away and not return
Where all the four winds blow
Please Mister President
Just go

A national risk that has been breached
Be you fired or impeached
Sacked, arrested, overthrown or simply just struck off
Two words Mr President
… Just go

Birthday Girl
#313 / 09:01:2021

Twenty-one years ago
You surprised us
By arriving early
Something you've rarely done since

But you keep surprising us
Always in a good way
With everything you've done
All your achievements

So much to be proud of
So much to be thankful for
You are the gift that keeps on giving
How did you get to be twenty-one?

Always our little girl
Now a woman
Always in our hearts
Now and forever

We Just Want Some News That Is Good
#314 / 10:01:2021

There's a madman in the White House
Whose hands are stained with blood
We just want some news that is good

COVID deaths keep rising
Just like we knew they would
We just want some news that is good

This Brexit Carry On show
That no-one understood
We just want some news that is good

All the lockdown guidelines
Looking clear as mud
We just want some news that is good

Those in power haven't done
As much as they all should
We just want some news that is good

The Queen has a got a vaccine
Like my granny never could
We just want some news that is good

Underfunded NHS
Teachers misunderstood
We just want some news
We just want some news
We just want some news that is
Better

On Reflection
#315 / 11:01:2021

It started off as something to fill the time
Time that had been taken away
Time performing, working, travelling
And suddenly – time at home

It began as a quirky habit
A little response to circumstances
Handwritten in a sketchbook
Shared here and there

Like the daily cartoons of Mr Riddell
A poetic response, a pun or a joke
At first for a few
Then it grew

And grew … and grew
This quirky habit became routine
Poetic daily exercises
Literal push ups and circuits

Encouraged by an online community
One audience lost
Another audience found
Immediate and inspiring

More than just exercise now
A daily committal
The fear of missing a day
In case I should just stop

I keep thinking "But what if …
What if there's nothing to write about?"
But there always is
The gift that keeps on giving

And here we are
Here we all are – still
Two-and-a-bit volumes later
And I've not run out of words

So we will continue
Onwards and upwards
This poetic communion
This breaking of breakfast together

One of you once wrote
"Your diary is our diary"
Poets are merely mirrors
And all poetry is but reflection

Asda Price
#316 / 12:01:2021

A food parcel at
Five pounds and twenty-two pence
Valued at thirty

Proving once again
Government figures don't add up
Just like this haiku verse

I bet you counted
Up all the syllables as well
Found more than seventeen

Just because I say
It's a haiku does not mean
That it is a haik

When Opportunity Knocks
There's Always A Tory Opportunist Waiting
#317 / 13:01:2021

Tory donors profiteering
You can almost hear them cheering
Rubbing hands with glee and jeering
Money that they're engineering
Whitehall sanctioned racketeering
Empty shallow sloganeering
Empathy is disappearing
Ordinary families fearing
Chartwell heartless commandeering
Ugly heads are always rearing
Eton pirates buccaneering
Tory donors profiteering

Today Is A Day For Unicorn Hats
#318 / 14:01:2021

The little girl in the unicorn hat
Skips in purple sparkly wellies
And is oblivious to the world

Holding hands with her mummy
And jumping in puddles
Is her entire world right now

The years that lie ahead
May be laden with worries
Seriousness and sadness

But that is not for now
Today is not a day for words like
"Pandemic" or "impeachment"

Today is a day for a unicorn hat
Splashing in puddles
And laughing

Jacob Rees Codd
#319 / 15:01:2021

A wet fish
Talks about wet fish
Being Brit-ish

The Girl In The Unicorn Hat ... Again
#320 / 16:01:2021

Yesterday, with the sudden heavy downfall of snow
I didn't go for my daily walk
And therefore didn't see the girl in the unicorn hat
I imagine a thicker coat and waterproof gloves
With the aforementioned hat and sparkly wellies
And the joy of the Christmas card canvas
The creation of snow angels
A snowball fight with mummy
And no doubt, the building of a snowman
The boys opposite built two
One fat, one thin
Both with the ubiquitous carrot noses
One has one long twig arm
The other has two short sticks
And no mouth
The lack of mouth is offset by the hair
Multicoloured drinking straws protrude
Crowning glory, genius
Today, it all looks a bit dirty
The roads have turned to slush
And the romance of snow is melting
And for now, the snowmen opposite still wave
One smiles while the other shows off his hair
A dozen tiny unicorn horns

This Time
#321 / 17:01:2021

This time it feels worse somehow
I mean, it is worse, much worse
Just look at the numbers ...

The first lockdown we had sunshine
Getting garden jobs done
Long walks, novelty and naivete

We didn't know how long it would really last
(Certainly not this long)
But we were somehow hopeful

Then there was the autumn
Lights at the end of tunnels
Some semblance of normality ...

And now this ... this
Christmas came and went miserably
No happy new year for anyone

We may have the vaccine
But things don't seem to be changing
Except for the worse

We are at that stage
Where we all know someone
Who is going through COVID – or hasn't

Everyone seems down, more resigned
As this poem seems to prove
In these darker depressed days

And that is why we need to reach out
Connect in whatever way we can
And just try to encourage one another

Sometimes
#322 / 18:01:2021

Sometimes the poems come easily
Trajectory from A to B

Sometimes the words flow readily
Almost as easy as one, two, three

A gift of a headline, a minister's quote
A pun in waiting, an obvious joke

The lines and rhymes fall into place
The punchline bides its time and waits

Yes, sometimes the poems come easily
Sometimes the words flow readily

And other times …
They don't

Of Course It Should Have Happened Nine Months Ago
But Don't Expect Common Sense From This Lot –
Anyway Here's A Limerick
#323 / 18:01:2021

For nearly nine months they've ignored us
But now we're getting the orders
We waited and waited
The virus mutated
So now we're closing our borders

Four Million And Counting
#324 / 19:01:2021

Vaccinations
A shot in the arm
Literally
Metaphorically

Congratulations
To all who help prevent harm
Unequivocally
Categorically

Trump – The Man Who Followed Through
#325 / 20:01:2021
An apt haiku.

Your legacy, a
Skidmark on the underpants
Of democracy

"Amusing, challenging, encouraging, bringing us to tears and getting us to think." *Steve Thorpe*

When Poetry Ruled The World
#326 / 21:01:2021

On a day when free speech returned
Poetry ruled the world
On a day when history happened
Poetry spoke for the world

After years of meaningless words
Words of hate, division and confusion
Came words of healing, words of hope
Words of light and inclusion

Words that dare to reach out in love
Rooted in the past
But growing towards a future
Seeds of inspiration

Words of harmony, not harm
Wondrous, not wounding
Words aflame and unafraid
Beautiful and brave

The voice of youth
That voiced the thoughts of all ages
The voice a minority
That spoke for a majority

And, not for the first time
The voice that spoke out loud and proud
Had a dream
And dared to dream that dream for all to hear

The voice of one
That spoke for the many
Amanda Gorman
Thank you for your words

Against All The Odds
#327 / 22:01:2021

In the face of crisis
The pressure unrelenting
Against all odds – you do your job

Life in your hands
Death at your fingertips
Against all odds – you do your job

You watch hopes rise
Then watch them fall
Against all odds – you do your job

You carry the weight of us all
Your own burden, even heavier
Against all odds – you do your job

You are tired yet do not sleep
Weary, yet you carry on
Against all odds – you do your job

When you cry
You cry for everyone
Against all odds – you do your job

Your mortuaries are filling
Yet your hearts are draining
Against all odds – you do your job

You do what has to be done
Because it simply has to be done
Against all odds – you do your job

Day upon day, week upon week
Month upon month
Against all odds – you do your job

Frontline fears, frontline tears
Against all the odds – you just do your job

One R.E.M. Song Comes To Mind
#328 / 23:01:2021

Watching the news does not give hope
A hundred thousand is not a number to be nearing
New Mutant Strain is not an album title or band name
Virus deniers do not speak the truth
Right now is not a time when optimism grows
But feels like life will never be the same again
One R.E.M. song comes to mind as it does indeed
Feel like the end of the world as we know it
But we don't feel fine

Sidetracked By A Song
#329 / 24:01:2021
'Start Again' by The Lottery Winners ft. Frank Turner.

Sometimes a cherished favourite
From a distant, different time
One that hits every single note
Emotionally as well as musically

Occasionally something new
An instant hit of joy
Out of the blue
Fresh, vibrant, uplifting – and more

All connection and goosebump moments
Restoring faith in the power of music
Redemption and joy in discovering a band
Who will be a friend for life

Already my day feels so much better
Played it three times back-to-back
And the smile hasn't left my face
Sidetracked by a song – totally

And what a song!
Knocked for six
Now it's here forever, a classic
A joyful noise indeed

No Poem Today
#330 / 25:01:2021

I look at the clock
Been up hours
Blank notepad page
Still not written today's poem

Had my daily walk
Had breakfast
One cup of tea, one cup of coffee
Still no poem today

Finding other things to do
Washing last night's pots
Rearranging books and papers
But still no poem today

Wandering around the house
Aimless pointless pottering
Easily distracted by old magazines
Yes, still no poem today

One of those days
Can't just seem to get going
No real focus to the day
Still no poem today

Opening lines appear, then fade
Nothing really sticks or takes
Maybe today will be the day
When there is no poem today

On the other hand
Perhaps this will have to do
Just one of those days
Sorry, didn't mean to let you down

Cheap Joke Alert, Feel Free To Move On ...
#331 / 26:01:2021
This is not really a poem, but it does rhyme ... sort of.

Sizzle! Sizzle! Hiss! Hiss! Ouch!
Can you see where this is goin'?
Whoosh! Ah! Oooh! Ow! Aaaaargh!
... Just my Burns Night poem

The Whole Story
#332 / 27:01:2021

It is not a day for light relief and puns
But heavy reflection

One hundred thousand as a number
Just does not tell the whole story

Over a million hours of life gone
Wembley Stadium ... and then some

A hundred thousand stories
None with happy endings

Touching hundreds of thousands more
With no chance of happy ever after

And a man who says
He is "deeply sorry for every single life lost"

And I do believe him
But he also says

"We truly did everything we could"
This I cannot believe

It does not tell the whole story

Proper Jobsworth
#333 / 27:01:2021

Good to go
Fit for purpose
I'm the man who signs the papers
Without me – everything stops
Simple as. Because I say so.
Simple as that.
Proper jobsworth, that's me.

Diligent
Rigorous to a point
But you have to be
A real pen pusher ...
Well, clipboard and very sharp pencil
If I'm being accurate
And in my job, you have to be accurate
Some call me a jobsworth
But if a job's worth doing
It's worth doing well
And properly

So, I check everything
And I mean everything
The locks on the doors
The thickness of the walls
Whether rooms are airtight
Electric cables, switches ...
I mean we do don't want anyone in charge here
Getting any nasty shocks do we?

Plumbing's got to be just right
Every joint checked, double checked
Triple checked
The boilers and the pipes
The miles of pipes, nozzles and connections
Let's face it, we can't have unnecessary leakage
Unnecessary bleeding

And those rooms that store the gas
And there are a lot of them
Well, they need to be away
From innocent employees

Fire hazards
So
If I don't say yes
Everything could stop right now
And we can't have that
Health and safety is of paramount importance
Especially here
We don't want injuries
Safeguarding for staff

We must be efficient
We have a job to do
Targets to keep to
Timetables to follow
Deadlines to meet

And if a job's worth doing
It's worth doing well
But – you've got to have checks
And I'm the man who signs the papers
Without me – everything stops. Simple as.
Because I say so. Simple as that.
Proper jobsworth, that's me.

Right. That's it. Passed.
Fit for purpose. Good to go.

Signed and dated:
Auschwitz 1941

I Truly Wrote Every Poem I Could
#334 / 28:01:2021

Looking now at poems I wrote
When all this first began
Am I happy with them now?
Do the images work and do they scan

Properly

What did I not write about?
Ignore – or just forget?
Did I misjudge or miss the point
Or plainly get it wrong – and, yet ...

It wasn't like they didn't work
I wrote what I thought at the time
But I could have worked on better structure
Sharper punchlines, better rhymes

Maybe used less humour
As the joke becomes the fixture
Led by puns and plays on words
Not the bigger picture

Delayed wisdom, hindsight
On all that's gone before
Of course, I'd write things differently
I could have written so much more

"Pithy, moving, amusing and occasionally heartbreaking ...
a must-read memento of these challenging times." *Paul Ross*

Actuality
#335 / 29:01:2021

I have written these poems
They do exist, printed out on paper
I can see them digitally shared
They are out there, somewhere
But now, with the book in my hands
They feel real, really real, real-er
Although that is not a real word
There is something about a book
That is always magical
Physical, actual, yes – magical
And permanently real
Open a book, you open a new world
Close a book, you close your minds
The thrill of turning pages, just holding it
Today, it's a real shot in the arm
And that will do for now

Unhappy Anniversary
#336 / 30:01:2021

30th January 2020
COVID deaths – one
One year on
Over 100,000 – gone

Straight To The Point
#337 / 31:01:2021

The fear of needles abates
A vaccine nation awaits
And appreciates
Inoculation rates

Sunshine Escapes From Doncaster

#338 / 01:02:2021
Even in these times, travel companies are sending emails about holidays!
I received one with this poem's title as its subject heading.

Just one chance is all it takes
The clouds collide, it makes its break
The sunshine makes its great escape
You could not plan it faster
It's begun – there goes the sun
Escaping from Doncaster

Sunshine escapes from Doncaster
Is what the brochure says
This lack of shine – not the best line
To sell these dark and dreary days
This monochrome metropolis
With fifty shades of greys
Certainly no summer sizzle
No happy ever after
It's all wrong – the sunshine's gone
Escaping from Doncaster

No time for topping up the tan
Don't get out the caravan
Every woman, every man
With skin like alabaster
It's no fun – there goes the sun
Escaping from Doncaster

Sunshine escapes from Doncaster
No taking in the rays
It's gone to find the nicer climes
On which to brightly blaze
The sun has put his hat on
And gone on holidays
There's no hips and no hoorays
It's cooler than Alaska
Minus one – without the sun
Escaping from Doncaster

Goodbye Yorkshire – time to go
Say hello to Mexico
Sithee Donny – dun't tha know
Best go to Madagascar
On the run – the convict sun
Escaping from Doncaster

Sunshine escapes from Doncaster
On a daily basis
There's nowt to put a smile upon
Those pallid Yorkshire faces
Eternally nocturnal – just one of those places
The land that time forgets – a natural disaster
Shadows long, no light upon
No sunshine's shone, the sunshine's gone
All said and done it's farewell sun
Escaping from Doncaster

**We Are All Blinkered
Until We Turn Around
And Look Back**
#339 / 02:02:2021

Hindsight is easy
Like wisdom in retrospect
We are all experts

Remembered in Perpetuity
#340 / 03:02:2021

An icon – passed on
A hero – now gone
Example – that shone
Thank you – Sir Tom

A legacy – strong
Second – to none
Our favourite son
Thank you – Sir Tom

So much to take from
Inspiration – begun
Life's a walk – not a run
Thank you – Sir Tom

His story – long
Touched everyone
For all you have done
We salute you – Sir Tom

Long live Sir Tom

Dear Oh Dear, Prime Minister ...
#341 / 04:02:2021

Please do not ask us to clap for Sir Tom
Applause for five minutes and then we move on
Instead, you could honour his legacy
By funding the NHS – properly
When charity's needed, something's not working
He did the job that you have been shirking
That public goodwill for his selfless action
Please do not use it as a distraction
Thank you Sir Tom – from all of us
Now where is the cash from the side of that bus?

Just Because You're On The Left
Doesn't Mean You're Always Right
#342 / 05:02:2021

Right wings means extremism
But … it's different on the left
Principles, core values
More important than the rest
Justice always on your side
Fighting the good fight
Just because you're on the left
Doesn't mean you're always right

No compromise! No compromise!
You stick with what you think
But others have to compromise
When you won't budge an inch
Ignoring double standards
As you bark and bite
Just because you're on the left
Doesn't mean you're always right

There's an even bigger picture
Two sides to every story
You can't just hate somebody
Because they voted Tory
It's not a case of wrong or right
Never black and white
Just because you're on the left
Doesn't mean you're always right

Too middle ground, too soft, too toff
Too weak to be electable
You just change your stereotypes
For ones you deem acceptable
He wears a suit, stands by a flag
A sir who's erudite …
Just because you're on the left
Doesn't mean you're always right

You'd rather fight amongst yourselves
Than join and win as one

Rather be a footnote
Than a chapter new, begun
Blinkered by self-righteousness
Blinded by your light
Just because you're on the left
Doesn't mean you're always right

You say you want democracy
But is that really true?
You won't accept and won't agree
With those opposing you?
You think you have the moral ground
And look down from your height
Just because you're on the left
Doesn't mean you're always right

A broad church and broad brush strokes
That's the here and now
The devil's in the detail
They'll make it there somehow
Don't dwell on past failures
When the future ain't so bright
Just because you're on the left
Doesn't mean you're always right

Reclaim the middle ground that's lost
Build up the trust from there
Change is one step at a time
Not halt and about turn
Don't shoot yourselves in the foot
Be long term with your sight
Just because you're on the left
Doesn't mean you're always right

If there is an enemy
It's not the one within
Shooting down your own
Will never be the way to win
Democracy is numbers cast
Each election night
Just because you're on the left
Doesn't mean you're always right

Don't Mess With Jackie Weaver
#343 / 06:02:2021

You have no authority here!
Well … now you'd better believe her
Just one click – you've disappeared
Don't mess with Jackie Weaver

Read the standing orders woman!
You don't need to be a reader
You're not in charge when she's at large
Don't mess with Jackie Weaver

It all kicked off in Handforth
Next time boys – just leave her
And if she wants to be Britney Spears
All power to Jackie Weaver

No nonsense and straightforward
Certainly no diva
Unlikely star – now go unleash
Your inner Jackie Weaver

I Wanted This To Be A Much Longer Poem
But Given The Subject Matter Could Only Manage Two Lines
And They Only Just Rhyme
#344 / 07:02:2021

Hats off to the government for ordering all the vaccine
Everything else … far too taxing

"All Over Fifties To Be Vaccinated By May" Claims Minister
#345 / 08:02:2021
A two-verse haiku, if you're interested.

I thought she'd retired
Didn't know she was helping
Out the NHS

After the way she
Was PM though, I'm not sure
I'd trust Theresa

Everything's Gone Sci-Fi
#346 / 09:02:2021

Everything's gone sci-fi
A variant mutation
A COVID strain from Kent
Attacking vaccination

Everything's gone Star Trek
E484K
Where's Captain Kirk
To help us save the day?

Everything's illogical
Everything is wrong
No ground control
No Major Tom

Life as we know it now
In twenty twenty-one
Feels like the future
To infinity and beyond

Mary Wilson – Voice Of An Angel
#347 / 10:02:2021
for Mary Wilson

One of three – the trinity
Wholly timeless legacy
Mary Wilson – voice of an angel

Royalty – sequinned queen
Love will always reign supreme
Mary Wilson – voice of an angel

Trail blazer, soul sister
Ground breaker, balance shifter
Mary Wilson – voice of an angel

Role model, perfect style
Superstar, winning smile
Mary Wilson – voice of an angel

Heart lifter, joy bringer
Always more than just a singer
Mary Wilson – voice of an angel

Perfect sounds – a guarantee
Part of Motown history
Mary Wilson – voice of an angel

Love was here – now you're gone
Forever we will sing along ... with
Mary Wilson – voice of an angel

I Just Can't Seem To Do It In My Slippers
#348 / 11:02:2021

Home-time showtime looming
My back bedroom zooming
Strange but true but my secret tip is
With high energy poetry
Something awkward seems to be
I just can't seem to do it in my slippers

Truth be told I have to choose
Converse or some indoor shoes
Feeling different I just get the jitters
Feeling somewhat incomplete
With nowt substantial on my feet
I just can't seem to do it in my slippers

They may be comfy, may be warmer
Too casual for a performer
Perhaps I need to find some winklepickers
Or something like them that would gauge
The feeling that I'm on a stage
I just can't seem to do it in my slippers

Change of shirt before I start
Checked that I just look the part
Checked my trousers, buttons and my zippers
Never thought it would be taxing
Just a case of too relaxing
I just can't seem to do it in my slippers

Try and try as I might
Something doesn't feel quite right
Like playing football in a frogman's flippers
What you see when I'm on show
You never know what's way down low
I just can't seem to do it in my slippers

So, Zoom or Teams or Google meet
You will never see my feet
Even if they smell like last week's kippers

Perpetuate an illusion
But it is my one conclusion
It may seem nothing to it
Only me who knew it
You hadn't got a clue it
Was a secret and I blew it
But I just can't seem to do it in my slippers

Cinquain Friday
#349 / 12:02:2021
A cinquain is a five-line poem with the syllable structure 2, 4, 6, 8, 2.

i. **No, I Don't Know How It's Pronounced Either**

Cinquain
Being succinct
In poetic form or
Just being too lazy to write
Much more?

ii. **Vac-cinquain-ation**

Not one
For violence
But I must admit I
Look forward to getting shot in
The arm

Far Too Soon To Think About A Summer Holiday
#350 / 12:02:2021

Rolling out the vaccine doesn't mean it's time
To think about the future when the sun is going to shine
There's still a killer virus and it hasn't gone away
Far too soon to think about a summer holiday

Don't pack your suitcase yet, your flip flops or your shorts
Don't browse the brochures – picking out resorts
Moderna's no taverna on the beach where you may stay
Far too soon to think about a summer holiday

BioNTech is no airline that is flying you to Pfizer
And Astra Zeneca's no Greek island either
Novavax is not a spray to keep the bugs at bay
Far too soon to think about a summer holiday

Something to look forward to, something to be planned
Sunshine, sea, sangria and sand
You want to book the tickets just praying it's okay
Far too soon to think about a summer holiday

We sing-a-long-a-Cliff – but none of it is true
We're not going anywhere for a year or two
Reasons to be cheerful – not many anyway
Far too soon to think about a summer holiday

Locked down lowdown, no-one goes abroad
Dreaming of a holiday instead of getting board
We can't all go to Cornwall – whatever some may say
Far too soon to think about a summer holiday

One Day
#351 / 13:02:2021

One day this will be a memory
That time we will never forget
When the world changed forever

One day this will be over
Eventually another page in history
Time will always move on

One day things will be different again
We will meet, laugh, hug, cry
All things must pass

One day this will all change
But not today, tomorrow
Next week or next month

But one day

Valentine
#352 / 14:02:2021

This poem is a virtual valentine
Words of love
A written hug to pass around
For the ones we haven't seen
Haven't held, haven't touched
All those we are distanced from

Mum – all those miles away
Grandad in the care home
A loved one in a hospital bed
Self-isolating fathers
Shielding grannies
Lonely brothers and solitary sisters

Nieces and nephews, uncles and aunts
Grandchildren – great and otherwise
The cousins you were once crazy with
Regular mates on regular dates
Friends you just hung around with
Acquaintances you'd always smile at

We want so much more than cards with hearts
More than a note with kisses
Roses and chocolates are not enough today
We look forward to the days
When hugs and embraces are not only possible
But compulsory and mandatory

The currency of communication
The language of connection
The warmth of contact and the silence of love
But until then
This virtual valentine will have to do
Share it, pass it on

Kenning For A Monday
#353 / 15:02:2021

Hair sculptor
Fib teller
Hand waver
Orange feller

Arrogance chooser
Loud shouter
Graceless loser
Nonsense spouter

Fake-news spreader
Riot inciter
Crowd stirrer
Democracy fighter

Truth avoider
Tax dodger
Vote ignorer
Complaint lodger

Result deny-er
Odds defy-er
Baby cry-er
Proven liar

Jeer leader
Congress traitor
Mob addresser
Dic tator

Don't Let Gran Near The Pancake Pan

#354 / 16:02:2021

Chaos in the kitchen always ensues
When Granny comes round every Shrove Tues-
Day when things don't go to plan
Don't let Gran near the pancake pan

Pancake batter mix – not quite right
Much too heavy when it should be light
Eggs, flour and – All Bran?!
Don't let Gran near the pancake pan

She says that it's not her fault
Adds some pepper and then some salt
Chilli sauce and strawberry jam!
Don't let Gran near the pancake pan

Milk and sugar, honey and cheese
Mustard, custard, curry and peas
Whisk in whisky, spam and ham
Don't let Gran near the pancake pan

Everything is tossed up high
It's all squashed as she lets fly
Mum disappeared and Dad just ran
Don't let Gran near the pancake pan

Windows, ceiling, tables, floor
Splattered more across the floor
Blocked up the extractor fan
Don't let Gran near the pancake pan

More lethal and dangerous than
King Kong fighting Jackie Chan
We all think that we should ban
Don't let Gran
Don't let Gran
Don't let Gran near the pancake pan

**It All Depends
On Your Point Of View**
#355 / 17:02:2021

Haven't
They
All done very well
They think that they have
Done their very best, they claim
With leadership they think is great
In unprecedented times
Boris and his merry band
As usual, they have failed us
Back to front and upside down
Totally the wrong way round
Read it from the last line up and you will see the truth

Filling The Empty Spaces
#356 / 18:02:2021

Yesterday
Was mostly about measurements
Angles, positioning, calculations
And precision

Down a bit
A smidge to the left
Up a touch
More …

A tape measure,
Very faint pencil,
Hammer, tacks
And a cheap spirit level

Getting it just right
Always takes longer
Yet we are glad of the focus,
This welcome distraction

A blank space on a wall
Filled with family
Special holiday memories
Or just something nice to look at

This is sufficient for today
Sometimes it is the mundane
That helps to ease
The day-to-day mundanity

No-One's Going On A Summer Holiday
#357 / 19:02:2021

Vacation, Staycation
Call it what you will
Chance of a holiday
Still nil

Two Saturday Cinquain Questions
#358 / 20:02:2021

In the
Midst of death and
Pandemic wouldn't it
Be ironic to find there's life
On Mars?

Also
Does it come as
A surprise to find out
That a minister has broken
The law?

One Of The Chosen ... Phew
#359 / 21:02:2021

Part relief, part belief
All part of being a blue
Far too long – at last we won
Liverpool nil – Everton two

Let The Teachers Teach
#360 / 22:02:2021

Affronted by fronted adverbials – I don't really know what they do
What's more, I don't really care and honestly – neither do you
Wasting time on useless terms that no-one really, really needs
Paperwork, targets and records are not the things to help us succeed

Assessment is just harassment – unnecessary and stress
Your teachers know just where you are … no one needs another test
When you're five you should feel so alive – looking to new discovery
The world is exciting and wild and wide … not grammatical recovery

Let the infants draw and paint – the juniors, draw and paint too
Build and mould and stick and make – co-operation be their glue
Lose yourself in language – let stories carry you further away
Just don't mention comprehension – destined to darken any day

Let poems and poets inspire you – the rhythm, the cadence and rhyme
Repetition – repetition – line after line after line
The repetition and repetition – line after line after line
Line after line after line after …

You don't need to understand or know – all the reasons behind
Just enjoy the feel of the words – time after time after time
Let enquiring minds be free to inquire – fan the flames and fuel the fire
Free to search and to inspire – *that* makes education higher

It's time there was a returning – the how and why, what and when
The simple love of learning – inspiring women, courageous men
The wonders of all creation – science and all of its mystery
Civilisations far and wide – the stories within all history

The acrobatics of mathematics – numbers and how they entrance us
The human urge for questions and the thirst for finding the answers
But you suck the joy and the lifeblood from learning like a leech
Vampire dementor committees – just let the teachers teach

Yes, let the teachers teach – not practise what a government preach
Out of touch and out of reach – just let the teachers teach
Celebrate inquisition – not subjunctive preposition
Drama, music and the arts – knowledge for the souls and hearts

Friendship and community – sport and teamwork in PE
A team, a cast that works together – those memories will last forever
The gift of life-loving learning should be given and shared unto each
Don't crucify enthusiasm – just let the teachers teach

Open up those deafened ears – we ask you, we beseech
It's common sense not nonsense – let the teachers teach
From whisper to frustrated screech – impassioned – we all impeach
Let's have freedom in our speech – just let the teachers … teach

**If The Prime Minister Was The Rhyme Minister
It Might Have Gone Like This...**
#361 / 23:02:2021

The crocus of hope is poking through the frost
And spring is on its way
The sunflower of confusion bends in the wind
With something important to say

At last – the end is really in sight
There may be a tunnel but now there is light
So now we've got a destination
Because of the roll out vaccination

The odds have shifted in our favour
This season of hope is something to savour
No credible route to a Zero COVID World
But my four-step plan has been unfurled

It could be all over by the end of June
Normal life could then resume
Incomparably better – we will not go back
Data not dates though, guiding this track

On a one-way road to freedom
Well, that's the truth that I'm believin'
I won't say too much – in case I'm shot down
This is my roadmap out of lockdown

A map – at last – you have my word
Alas – no atlas – and slightly blurred

A Reason To Put My Trousers On
#362 / 24:02:2021

Most days are pyjama days
No reason to head out at all
Not so splendid isolation
Stuck inside the same four walls
But today I have a meeting
Zoom at half past one
Giving me a reason
To put my trousers on

Another day I didn't shave
No going out to work
Another day in slippers
And the same old shirt
Google meeting in a school
Best not get it wrong
Giving me a reason
To put my trousers on

Book case right behind me
In my back bedroom
It's only head and shoulders
When it's Teams or Zoom
But I don't want to stand up ...
Shocking everyone
Giving me a reason
To put my trousers on

I'm watching too much football now
And all sorts of sports
Doesn't mean that I have to
Walk around in shorts
No-one needs to see my knees
Or cast their gaze upon ...
Giving me a reason
To put my trousers on

No-one needs to see my socks
Given half a chance
Even less than that
When it comes to underpants
Should I choose the Y-fronts
Or that purple thong?
Giving me a reason
To put my trousers on

Serial Filler
#363 / 24:02:2021

Too much milk
Too little cereal
Vice vera

Do you add more cereal?
Drink the milk?
Or just pour it away?

Muesli is the worst
You think you've got it right
Then find it has drunk the milk

Hindsight Time Machine
#364 / 25:02:2021

A Hindsight Time Machine
Would a jolly fellow make
I'd build a factory making masks
And green and yellow tape

The Heart Of Giving Thanks
#365 / 25:02:2021

Thanks to all friends – near and far
Those I've known for years, met before
Those who have connected on line
I feel I know you all

I've missed the shows, performing
But your daily comments
Your virtual applause and encouragement
Have really kept me going

Really. You say my words brighten your day
Well, your words do that and more
And if it wasn't for them
I may well have stopped by now

But I haven't – as this poem proves
You have given me responsibility
A daily purpose and challenge
Allowing me to flex this pen

And one day – one day
When this war is over
We will all gather in the same room
And share our words together

There will be laughter – lots
Hugs and wine and probably pies
And as one we share the First Supper
Of many more to come

And, of course
Should there be time
After all the above
There may well be poetry

Day For A Light Coat
#366 / 26:02:2021

For the first time this year
It was a day for a light coat
No gloves, hat or scarf
But a light coat and a tee shirt

No jumper for my daily walk
Of course, the postmen were in shorts
But aren't they always?
Me, I felt better in a light coat

Sunshine, warmth
And the first smell of fresh cut grass
Things felt almost normal
And somehow better in the world

All because of a light coat and sunlight
So I didn't put the news on
Didn't want to spoil things
Or feel depressed

So I put the Test Match on instead
But obviously not for long
Not wanting to feel depressed
I put on my light coat again

And walked in the sunshine

High ... Cool
#367 / 27:02:2021

Full snow moon shines bright
Perfect pearl in the oyster
Of God's sky at night

Mint imperial
The best, saved to last, Heaven's
Immortal sweet box

Because You Were A Robin
#368 / 28:02:2021

Because you were a robin
You got away with it

Sunshine and warmth made me do it
The red padded chair from the outside den
Sat on the patio for a few minutes
While I rearranged furniture

Not two yards away, within seconds
You quickly landed and perched
Perhaps drawn by the colour
I very nearly tried to take a snapshot

Then you looked my way, chirped
Left your dirty mark
And flew skywards
Your small white worm on my chair

Had you been a sparrow or blackbird
The one for sorrow magpie, or even worse
The pigeon that keeps Jackson Pollocking the fence
It would have been different

So very different
Shoes would have been thrown
Curses uttered
Alongside dreams of shotgun target practise

But because you were a robin
Probably the same one that watched me
When I painted the fence last summer
You got away with it

Cheeky

I've Always Been A Pie Sort Of Guy
#369 / 01:03:2021
for National Pie Week

I've always been a pie sort of guy
It doesn't matter how hard I may try
My trust is in the crust
The pastry that is puffed
And the filling guaranteed to satisfy

I've always been a pie sort of guy
A fact my waistline just cannot defy
Ingredients – terrific
And oh so calorific
All the things I just cannot deny

I've always been a pie sort of guy
As my taste buds all will testify
Gloriously flavoury
Gravy oh so savoury
Causing senses to intensify

I've always been a pie sort of guy
As the words of this verse now signify
The beauty and the bake
The kidney and the steak
The taste of which, we all can just rely

I've always been a pie sort of guy
No mincing of my words will now apply
The faith and the belief
In everything that's beef
The relief of demand and then supply

I've always been a pie sort of guy
Like a giant I fee and fo and fi
Aroma so distinctive
To me it's just instinctive
Who could resist it? No, not I

I've always been a pie sort of guy
And I spy with my little eye

That even the vegan
Is now well worth receiving
Not averse to then diversify

I've always been a pie sort of guy
The appeal of which, let nobody decry
I'll talk and then I'll talk
Of the jelly and the pork
These blessings, well they all just multiply

I've always been a pie sort of guy
No mystery to de-mystify
Potato, meat or chicken
The pot will always thicken
And my pulse will always quicken my oh my!

Lots of people seem to question why
Why it is that I would glorify
This genius combination
This simple taste sensation
I've always been a pie sort of guy

Tanka Time
#370 / 02:03:2021

Anger and duvet
Covers do not mix at all
I hoover in straight
Lines like when I mow the lawn
One sock absconds each wash day

Once A Saint, Always A Saint
#371 / 03:03:2021
for Ian St John

Some players are catalysts
Turning points and vital cogs

Goal scorers and heroes
Timeless icons

You were one such player

With Greavesie
Saturday lunchtimes brightened

Warmth, humour
Knowledge and gravitas

Some players transcend rivalries
Some players ooze class

Football may divide us
But ultimately it unites us

You were one such player

Once a saint, always a saint
Ian Saint John

The Mysterious World Of Numbers ...
Or Four Reasons Why I Will Never Be Chancellor
#372 / 04:03:2021

Not good with numbers at all
I'm easily confused

Borrowing billons in a financial crisis
At what point do they become meaningless?

It is a mystery to me
I really have no idea

     1.   Where we are actually borrowing it from
     2.   Who actually has it in the first place

And

     4.   Whether it all adds up

Hell Bent
#373 / 05:03:2021

One year on the front line – heroes heaven sent
Central to resistance – those on whom we've leant

Clapping on our doorsteps was your main event
Your gratitude – just platitudes – you think they're so well meant

Now we've had the budget that shows your real intent
NHS ... one per cent

Priorities
#374 / 06:03:2021

Billions for contracts that your friends can all supply
Millions awarded to those you justify
Thousands for a court case as the numbers testify
Funding for a flat that you want to beautify

You could have paid the nurses more but didn't really try
An act of public spending that no-one would decry
This evidence on show would seem to signify
That it's crystal clear where priorities may lie

But questions stay unanswered with all that you deny
All anybody wants is a straightforward reply
Priority's majority – and it's no surprise
That this is where priorities lie

Or this is where priority is lies

Another Poem Banging The Same Drum
#375 / 07:03:2021

Rewarding frontline workers
The ones who've helped us through it
You could have been a hero
And still you couldn't do it

Hollow words and clapping
We know there's nothing to it
You had a chance to do what's right
And once again you blew it

Catch Up
#376 / 08:03:2021

Catch up with your teachers
Catch up with your class
Catch up with the gossip
Catch up with the laughs

Catch up with your friends
Catch up with your buddies
Catch up with each other first
Then ...
Catch up with your studies

Royal Family Matters
#377 / 09:03:2021

The Royal Family
Seem to be getting upset
That some members of
The Royal Family
Are talking publicly about
The Royal Family
Apart from one member of
The Royal Family
Who is probably glad that others in
The Royal Family
Are discussing secrets of
The Royal Family
And therefore not other alleged secrets in
The Royal Family

TV Tantrums And Tiaras On The End Of The Piers Show
#378 / 10:03:2021

There is fall out from the fall out
A media debacle
Hissy fits, a bully quits
Because of Meghan Markle

Recollections – They May Vary
#379 / 11:03:2021

Who said what, to whom and when – evidentially contrary
Dates and times and places, recollections – they may vary

Deal with it internally, be vigilant and wary
Question all suggestions but recollections – they may vary

Catastrophic fall out, consequences – scary
Just who is accountable when recollections – they may vary

Accusations hanging, we can't be judged unfairly
Tread carefully and do our best but recollections – they may vary

Face up to valid questions, answer – fair and squarely
It's only right and proper but recollections – they may vary

Hurtful allegations, mentioned – only barely
Damage limitations as recollections – they may vary

Replies and repercussions, one thinks about it rarely
Best that we say nothing as recollections – they may vary

We'd like less from the Duchess and as for the Prince, how dare he?
When all is said and all is done, recollections – they may vary

Recollection – variable, subjective in selection
Memory and reflections, not facts – just recollection

I Bid You Not

#380 / 12:03:2021

When looking at news headlines online I came across an article suggesting Winston Churchill's slippers could be auctioned for £15,000 ... the rest ... made up ... or are they?

Winston Churchill's slippers
Margaret Thatcher's toenail clippers
Harold Macmillan's flippers
Tony Blair's Panini stickers

Mussolini's loofah
Che Guevara's shaving foam
Adolf Hitler's underpants
Denis Healey's comb

Hermann Göring's rubber duck
Idi Amin's Stickle Bricks
Ronald Reagan's tuba
Norman Tebbit's cycle clips

Fidel Castro's feather boa
Robert Mugabe's foot spa
Clement Attlee's tap shoes
Pinochet's guitar

Lenin's ukulele
Stalin's cricket bat
Arthur Scargill's cummerbund
Gorbachev's cravat

Gaddafi's balaclava
Richard Nixon's snooker cue
Jeremy Thorpe's surgical support
Kenneth Clarke's corkscrew

Mahatma Gandhi's banjo
The Ayatollah's football socks
Winston Churchill's slippers
I bid and kid you not

I Feel Like I May Be Going On A Bit About This Now But ...
#381 / 13:03:2021

Money on buses that does not exist
Just remember – you voted for this

A chance for a hit – and still they all miss
Just remember – you voted for this

Difficult times – yes it is what it is
Just remember – you voted for this

You might want to boo – you might want to hiss
Just remember – you voted for this

You chose to stick – when it could have been twist
Just remember – you voted for this

The natural order of things must persist
Just remember – you voted for this

NHS – that Judas Kiss
Just remember – you voted for this

Tory party – just taking the ...
Just remember – you voted for this

Accidental Beard

#382 / 14:03:2021

The beard that started accidentally
Is still here, after a year

A casual decision not to shave
"Until all this is over"
Thinking we'd be back to normal in no time
And yet, here we are ...

Now an artistic statement
Whatever that may mean
Well, I say "artistic"
It looks like I've dipped my chin in whitewash

So, the year of the beard
And the question is
In approximate words sung by The Clash
Should it stay or should it go?

Or maybe go in stages ...
Leave the sideburns à la Noddy Holder
'Tache and Frank Zappa chin triangle
Freddie Mercury soup strainer
Or Oliver Hardy / Ron Mael gingerish Hitler

Maybe have it sculpted
By that, I mean shaped
Not cut in the shape of a topiary bird

Is it time to see my chin again?
Or do I leave it on until this madness
Really is all over

Could be a long time
I could end up auditioning as a
ZZ Top chin double

Three Short Poems For A Monday – Two Trivial, One Not
#383 / 15:03:2021

i. **Any Less And It Doesn't Work**

When suitably inspired for poetry that rhymes
The minimum requirement – at least two lines

ii. **Too Long To Be The Shortest But Just Right For A Haiku**

This was to be the
Shortest poem in the world
… Too long, already

iii. **Haiku**

If a vigil is
Needed then all of us need
To be vigilant

Spaffing Money
#384 / 16:03:2021

As an idea it's a silly 'un
Spending two point nine million
On a room just for briefing
It shows no belief in
Our nurses now worth a billion

Today's The Day I Have My Jab
#385 / 16:03:2021

All you Anti-Vaxxers
An argument? I'll start it
What's to disagree with?
Who wants a dirty carpet?

Step One
#386 / 17:03:2021

So
I've had the injection
Vaccination Step One complete
Didn't hurt a bit

No noticeable side effects
Although my satnav
Seemed to work much better
On the way home

Every time I lift my left arm
I change the TV channels
And I now seem to beep
When I walk backwards to the worktop

Apart from that – all okay
So thanks to the NHS
And Boris Johnson – leader of the Astra Zenicans
Doing a fantastic job job jobjobjobjobjobwibble

I Wandered Lonely As A Cow

#387 / 18:03:2021

"I wandered lonely as a cow" was allegedly Wordsworth's original first line.

I wandered lonely as a cow
That tramps on high o'er vales and hills
When all at once I saw a crowd
A host of golden daffodils
Beside the lake, beneath the trees
Fluttering and dancing in the breeze

Entranced was I by golden glow
Their shimmer shining in the sun
Hypnotised and drawn and so
I bit their heads off one by one
And oh to savour such a taste
I did not waver, did not waste

Ten thousand heads that glow no more
Ten thousand stalks of naked green
A banquet for this herbivore
A feast of riches seldom seen
Exquisite taste, much more than good
When all these days I chewed on cud

Such extra weight on leg and hoove
I staggered, churning from the field
Four stomachs full I scarce could moooove
Back to the farm to share my yield
Thus caused the milking maid to utter
I gave not milk but yellow butter

The Wild Goats Are Back On The Streets Of Llandudno
#388 / 19:03:2021
After I'd written this, I was informed that it was pronounced Llan-did-no
… but I'd written it by then.

They're filling the streets instead of the cars
Standing outside all the shops and the bars
Here is a fact that everyone should know
The wild goats are back on the streets of Llandudno

There's a storm from way up in Orme and quite clearly
It's the appearance of all these Kashmiri
The breed of these creatures that very few could know
The wild goats are back on the streets of Llandudno

Hedges and bushes and flowers and leaves
Nothing is safe from the munching of these
Beasts who are feasting on much more than wood though
The wild goats are back on the streets of Llandudno

Not just the greenery, blossoms and plants
Washing line thievery – dad's underpants
So much more than chewing the cud though
The wild goats are back on the streets of Llandudno

Invading the churches, the parks and the schools
Not acting the goat – they're nobody's fools
Just check your shoes for where you've been stood though
The wild goats are back on the streets of Llandudno

Sowing wild oats – it's natural selection
Thanks to COVID – no goat contraception
Could be a movie – not very good though
Return of the Goats to the Streets of Llandudno

The Prime Minister Answers Truthfully
#389 / 20:03:2021

At last an honest answer – truth that has a ring
"I literally did not feel a thing"

No little prick of anything, no tiny little sting
"I literally did not feel a thing"

In the kingdom of the blind, the one-eyed man is king
"I literally did not feel a thing"

It could be any question that he was answering
"I literally did not feel a thing"

One per cent for nurses – but a briefing room needs zing
"I literally did not feel a thing"

Carry on regardless – ignore the suffering
"I literally did not feel a thing"

Time To Channel My Inner Noddy Holder
#390 / 21:03:2021

It's time to begin again
Time to see my chin again
The year of the beard, weird – but now one year older
Couldn't shave it all at once
Why oh why? My response …
I think it's time to channel my inner Noddy Holder

Time to end the merriment
Of this beard experiment
File away the photos – in an unmarked folder
Father Christmas, ZZ Top?
No – I think it's time to stop
I think it's time to channel my inner Noddy Holder

Bye bye beard of white and grey
Sideburns though, well they may stay
I've never had the chance to look like Trevor Boulder
Or the opportunity
To look like you in seventy-three
I think it's time to channel my inner Noddy Holder

The ginger 'tache that I tried is
Now replaced by only sidies
Muttonchops ahoy – although my chin is colder
Like a character from Dickens
It isn't just the plot that thickens
I think it's time to channel my inner Noddy Holder

I may not have the shoes and flares
I may not have the Dave Hill hair
Young and wild and flowing free and resting on my shoulder
They may not be here to stay
But even if it's for a day
I can say I channelled my inner Noddy Holder

A COVID-19
#391 / 22:03:2021

After a year of writing a poem a day I can't believe I haven't thought of this earlier – a new poetic form. A haiku is 17 syllables, 5, 7, 5, so a COVID-19 is therefore 19 syllables, 6, 7, 6.

Just when we thought it was
Safe to swim again, here's death
Surfing on the third wave

No Words
#392 / 23:03:2021

There are no words
To fill one minute of silence
That do justice to those we have lost

There are no words
To explain the devastation
Or make sense of this time

There are no words
That sound anything other than glib
Clichéd or trite

There are no words
Of any use whatsoever in this poem
So I'll shut up

Cut From The Same Cloth These Days
#393 / 23:03:2021

I have lost trust in politicians
All of them, pretty much

However, reading that phrase
Implies I trusted some of them
Sometime

As a young man they all seemed to be
Older men who seemed to have "done something"
... as in had a real job
Before going into politics
So at least had some experience of real life

Even if you didn't agree with them
At least they had some sort of gravitas

Now
Most of them look the same
All too young
No experience of working life to guide them

Not about sides either
Just happens to be "them" at the moment
So we can't really judge the others

Apart from the fact
They seem ineffectual so far
Maybe they are just waiting

But this lot
The grey mafia of incompetence
The amorphous blob of ... nothingness

Two years ago
They must have thought they'd got it made
Landslide victory
Massive majority
Five years of easy pootling along

And then COVID
Bang
Lockdown
Boom

And here they are
Dithering
Wavering in the wind
Clueless and corrupt
Not a decision of note between them
All promoted beyond their means

So yes
I have lost faith in politicians
I've sworn at the telly daily
For a long, long time now
And I'm sick of it
Totally

I'm Not Wasting More Than Two Lines
On This Phrase That Shows His True Colours
And Tells Us Everything We Need To Know
#394 / 24:03:2021

Not a chance he's misunderstood
When he says "greed is good"

"Impressively cutting." *Janet Cuthbert*

Mortal Yet Immortal
#395 / 25:03:2021
for Peter Lorimer and Frank Worthington

Neither played for our teams of choice
But playing football every school playtime
Or on the rec every Saturday afternoon
We always wanted to be like you

Your names – not just football legends
Immortal to those of us of an uncertain age
But names that became verbs
Part of our everyday games

A power-blaster past the keeper
And we'd done a "Lorimer"
Keepy-uppies, a juggle, a twist, turn and shot
"Oh what a Worthington!"

Men defined by the perfect moments
They created, week in, week out
We defined ourselves by trying
To recreate those self-same moments

And those magical moments
Remind us of a different time
Not just when we were young
But when footballers were ordinary gods

Heroes? Yes
Superstars? Yes
Legends? Yes
But everyday ordinary blokes who were gods

Soon there will come a time
When we say
"They don't make them like they used to
Last of a dying breed ..."

Peter Lorimer and Frank Worthington
Mortal yet immortal
We thank you and salute you
And we will never forget

Anniversary Poem

#396 / 26:03:2021

I wrote my first poem of this series a year ago – after the first doorstep applause for the NHS – and when the project became a book, I went back and retrospectively wrote the first three poems to fit in with the concept.

A year ago today
I wrote a poem called 'Connection'
That may seem a strange admission from a poet
Writing a poem – but it isn't

There were days, weeks even
And I wouldn't write a new poem
I'd perform poems every day, all round the country
And – in doing so
Not have the time to write

Then that stopped. Overnight
Work disappeared. Changed
Time suddenly on my hands
As the world tilted on its axis

So, with nothing else to do
I wrote a poem
Then another
And another

I didn't know then
That it would become a daily occurrence
But it did
And it has

Neither did I know then
That it would turn into three books
Yes, three new books in one year
And nearly four hundred new poems

You have been my audience
Virtual applause on a daily basis
You have also been my inspiration
My encouragement and my purpose

Who knows what the future holds
But here we all are
Still writing
Still lots to write about

And long may we continue
In this daily communion
Whatever form it takes
Peace be with you

Shopping Malady
#397 / 27:03:2021

In the shopping centre
Four young men strut lazily
Flouting not only the one-way system
But also the request for face coverings

They are loud
And unaware of everyone else
Nobody says anything
No security asks them to cover up

So they do just what they want
As they want, regardless
I am glad of my own mask
They cannot hear the words I call them

Or if they do
They can't prove it

The Words Of Mother Abagail

#398 / 28:03:2021

Mother Abagail is a character in my favourite book, Stephen King's The Stand.

The words of Mother Abagail
Ringing like a bell
God has got great things for you to do
You say you don't believe in him
Well, that don't matter much
Why? ... He believes in you

Prophecy or heresy
Foolishness or lie
Or messages from heaven that are true?
Either way, you've got to make your choice
And take a stand
Why? ... He believes in you

Weasels in the cornfield
Rats are in the barn
Shadows that surround the chosen few
Oh ye of little faith
You will find the strength
Why? ... He believes in you

The words of Mother Abagail
Like a silent psalm
A prayer to hold as we're all passing through
The valley of the shadows
On to the other side
Why? ... He believes in you

Faith or hope or doubt
Truth or disbelief
God has still got things we all must do
In the words of Mother Abagail
All these things shall pass
Why? ... He believes in you

Just In Case You Thought I Was Ignoring Our Glorious Leader
#399 / 29:03:2021

Read the sordid stories if you must
Is this someone that we all can trust?

We Live In Hope
#400 / 30:03:2021

The sun shone brighter
Blue sky warmth and tee-shirt sleeves
My usual walk

Past the school at playtime
Invigorated by voices of happy children
Shouting, playing, laughing

And in that moment
It could be any time at all
Any year, not this one

Life being lived
Time being enjoyed
Long may it continue

If Boris Johnson Was Harry Carpenter
#401 / 31:03:2021
A cinquain – 5 lines, 2, 4, 6, 8, 2 syllables.

Jab jab
A quick one two
We've got it on the ropes
Winning the fight against COVID
Jab jab

Summery ... Or Summary?
#402 / 01:04:2021

The first day for shorts
And a longer walk
That takes me across the fields
And to the canal

Sun on my face
Birdsong in my ears
Not a human in sight
Alone apart from one brown duck

If I close my eyes and relax
I could be anywhere
Untroubled and carefree
Until I put my hand in my pocket

The mask is there ... waiting
A reminder that the bad times
Are not behind us
And normality a way off yet

One Consequence Is Of The Consequences
#403 / 02:04:2021

There is talk and fear
A third wave on the horizon
In these times of strangeness
Nothing's now surprising

Adapt, survive, continue
Carry on come what may
And even worse – you're cursed with verse
I'll have the time for a poem a day

**Measuring Life
In Multiples Of Seventeen**
#404 / 03:04:2021

I've started wearing
My watch again in the hope
That times are changing

And started to think
In seventeen syllables
A human haiku

Sun Rise Service
#405 / 04:04:2021

Easter Sunday in the seventies
Always started in the darkness

Members of our church would congregate
On the gentle slopes of Beacon Fell

As dawn broke we would sing hymns
Listen anew to resurrection stories

Then go back to the church hall
For bacon, eggs, beans and hot tea

The cold of the morning air
Watching darkness become light

Always brought things to life again
Seeing the sun actually rise

Sun rise
More than just play on words

Progress?
#406 / 05:04:2021

Now numbers are not at their peak
The future is looking less bleak
This road map to freedom
Shows how we're proceedin'
With two tests now every week

Countdown To Normal
#407 / 06:04:2021

Countdown to normal
We cannot wait for everyday routines
Desperate for the regular

Haircuts, shops and workouts
The communion of sport and art
Beer and restaurant tables

The little things we've missed
Bigger with each passing day
Absence makes the heart grow

So long we have been distant
Necessarily anti-social
Craving connection and contact

Countdown to normal
Proceed with caution
Not there yet

Some Days
#408 / 07:04:2021

Some days
I don't feel like writing poems
But I said I would
So here I am again
A man of my word
Sat at the dining room table
Notebook open
The fourth so far
(Notebooks that is, not tables)
And pen in hand
Looking for inspiration
Waiting for the magic
When mostly it isn't magic
But just following the trail of the words
As one leads to another
Then another
And another
Until we have this ...

A poem
Of sorts
That doesn't rhyme

If I Was You Mr Williamson
I Would Choose My Words Very Carefully
(As indeed I have when writing this two-verse haiku)
#409 / 08:04:2021

Oh the irony
Discipline and order show
Your double standards

How can a man in
Charge of education still
Remain ignorant?

Eternal Optimist
#410 / 09:04:2021

Two days of sunshine
Out came the shorts
Off came the beard
One week later
These actions seem premature
And somewhat foolish
I thought my hat and gloves
Had been banished
Until the autumn
Apparently not
Walking in the wind and snow
My chin is suddenly colder

Grief And Loss Are Grief And Loss
#411 / 10:04:2021

Someone's granddad died today
Someone's father passed away
Someone's husband – laid to rest
Someone loved – someone blessed
Private view, public glare
Ever present – always there
All the things we never saw
Behind the scenes, behind the door
Just like every family
Every day – a memory
A glance, a touch, a quip, a joke
Things he did and words he spoke
Human, flawed – the man he was
But grief and loss are grief and loss
Those who love are those who grieve
Those who mourn for those who leave
Those who leave who leave their mark
Are carried in each heavy heart
Love is love – come what may
Someone cherished – died today

Unguarded
#412 / 11:04:2021

In the midst of pomp and ceremony
A joke

In the midst of protocol and circumstance
A well-planned prank

A moment of surprise
A snapshot of lightness and humanity

You – the guard
Caught her – off guard

And her smile said everything
The Queen and her joker

A truly royal flush

Fling Wide The Doors
#413 / 12:04:2021

Open the gyms, the bars and the stores
Unlock the shops, fling wide the doors
Welcome back beers – sound the applause
Hooray for haircuts – fling wide the doors

A little normality – back on these shores
Head to the high street – fling wide the doors
Responsibility – take time to pause
Think about others – fling wide the doors

Don't be the reason – don't be the cause
For flinging wide open – hospital doors

The Business Of Buzzing Crowds
#414 / 13:04:2021

Like ants on an ice cream that's spilt on the floor
The madness of masses that gather galore
The swarming's a warning we should not ignore

Making the most of this new situation
Social and sunshine – a welcome elation
An over-reaction to long isolation …

Retail relief – the high streets are seething
It beggars belief – beer gardens heaving
Just what is the truth that we are believing?

The road map to freedom is already tattered
As personal freedom is all that has mattered
Let's hope that the virus hasn't been scattered …

Sign Of The Times
#415 / 14:04:2021

Gents so unkempt, they loiter in streets
Embarrassed – they gaze at their shoes
Waiting and watching – long-haired in the heat
It's the time for – barber queues

Stereotypes And Mixed Metaphors
#416 / 15:04:2021

It's true – we don't know all of the facts
It's true – we don't understand
What's also true – because it is you
It's probably underhand

One rule for the plebs and the peasants
A different one for the toffs
Stereotypes and mixed metaphors
Fat cat mates – snouts in troughs

Thick As Thieves
#417 / 16:04:2021

Cash for questions, cronyism – corruption guaranteed
Money talks and silences those who deal in greed
Truth has been a casualty ... nobody grieves

Why? Because you're all as
Thick as thieves

Transparency now clouded – lines are grey and blurred
Your mouths may be moving but we don't believe a word
Unopposed – ranks are closed – you do just as you please

Why? Because you're all as
Thick as thieves

Trust has been eroded – principles – well, none
Accountable for actions – disappeared and gone
You've got a code of conduct that nobody believes

Why? Because you're all as
Thick as thieves

We know that hands are dirty and pockets have been lined
No interest in an inquest – the only thing you'll find
Evidence of negligence? Nothing up your sleeves

Why? Because you're all as
Thick as thieves

No beginning and no end to all the Tory sleaze
Why? Because you're all as thick as thieves
There's no vaccination – no end to this disease

We must all be thick
And you are thieves

A Family
#418 / 17:04:2021

A family gathers to say goodbye
Private grief, public eye

A family gathers to pay respect
Recall, remember and reflect

A family gathers to say farewell
A life well-lived, a life lived well

A day for closure and release
Let a family grieve in peace

His Favourite Cap
#419 / 18:04:2021

His favourite cap
Always wore it
Never without it
Unless indoors
Loved it more
Than other hats he had to wear
More him, just him
At home, comfortable
His favourite cap
Fitting

Supermarket Flowers
#420 / 19:04:2021

For the second weekend running
I made the two-hundred-mile round trip
For a garden cup of tea with mum
Stopping only to buy supermarket cakes
And a bunch of flowers

She rang in the week
To tell me how beautiful they still are
And haven't they lasted well
No doubt she'll ring this week
And say the same about the cheap tulips

It's the little things
I suppose
We are making up for lost time
And time we may not always have

That
And still being able
To buy flowers
For the living

"Can't do without my daily fix." *Angela McDermott-Roe*

Spectacular Own Goal
#421 / 20:04:2021

It's all about the money
But this – a brand new low
European Super League
Not the way to go
By the few and for the few
It's remote control
The day that football sold its soul
Spectacular own goal

Out of touch and out of reach
Disregard for fans
Forget about the football
It's just financial plans
Digging down for further gold
Deepening the hole
The day that football sold its soul
Spectacular own goal

Tearing up remaining roots
Severing tradition
Ignoring all the history
That gave them this position
Blinkered and self-serving
No respect at all
The day that football sold its soul
Spectacular own goal

Not even based on merit
Just the chosen few
Blatant profiteering
Though that is nothing new
Complete and utter disregard
Just climb that greasy pole
The day that football sold its soul
Spectacular own goal

The grass that seems much greener
Means you will walk alone
As football is divided by
The green greed grass of home

All fans now united
Revolted on the whole
The day that football sold its soul
Spectacular own goal

Just Because
#422 / 21:04:2021

Just because what happened yesterday
Doesn't mean that the problem's gone away
Greed and football – here and here to stay

Just because the six have all retreated
Doesn't mean that greed has been defeated
Or that these mistakes will not be repeated

Just because the numbers now are thinning
Doesn't mean that people power is winning
Remember this – they signed up – when it was beginning

Just because it's now about to fail
Doesn't mean that it wasn't a betrayal
When everything it seems is always up for sale

Just because they tweet the tweets, making the right sound
Doesn't mean that they are standing on their moral ground
Common sense and honesty have only just been found

Just because you're backing out of this situation
Doesn't mean you're saving your tarnished reputation
Or that you should be exempt from recrimination

When somebody can earn a fee in just one day
The wages of a nurse who is on full pay
There'll never be a thing that we can call fair play

Just because – what happened yesterday
Doesn't mean that greed is going to go away
The game that once was beautiful – now, only just okay

A Step In The Right Direction
#423 / 21:04:2021

Yesterday was different
For the first time in months
I had to think about shoes
Actual shoes
Not slippers or trainers

Also, a button-up shirt
Not a tee shirt with a band name on

And a shave
Not beardy stubble
(Which could be a band name)

Yes, I was up early
And driving to Hull
To a favourite school

Back to work
For a day anyway

Today, back at home
Writing poems

And looking at the diary
No longer totally blank

Short And Sweet
#424 / 22:04:2021

I've got a daily poem to write
Before I do my weekly shop
Just got time – four lines that rhyme
Then I'd better stop

For England, Shakespeare And Saint George
#425 / 23:04:2021

Rule Britannia
Raise your glasses
For England, Shakespeare and Saint George

Fly the flag
Be proud of our heritage
For England, Shakespeare and Saint George

Gather solemnly, not in churches
But pub gardens
For England, Shakespeare and Saint George

Is this a lager I see before me?
To beer or not to beer?
That is the question

Charge your glasses
Toast our great country
And sing our anthem loud and proud

'ere we go – 'ere we go – 'ere we go

A Birthday Is Never A Birthday When So Close To A Funeral
#426 / 24:04:2021

Apparently
I missed your birthday
What with everything else going on
It slipped under my radar
Not that I've ever sent you a card
And even if I did
There's no certainty it would reach you
Or that you would read it
But it must have been a strange one
Your first alone after all this time
So even if I'd sent a card
It wouldn't have included the word "Happy"
I can only hope that it passed unremarkably
Ma'am

It's Coming To Something When ...
#427 / 25:04:2021

The man who can't be trusted
On a man who can't be trusted
Has come back done and dusted
For the man who had him busted

Get Some Sense of Perspective ...
Or Just Get Some Sense
#428 / 26:04:2021

India – tens of thousands die
As COVID keeps on breeding
London – thousands march and shout
About their personal freedom

Let The Bodies Pile Up High
#429 / 27:04:2021

Let nature take its natural course
Let's live and then let die
I'm Bond and COVID's Blofeld
Let the bodies pile up high

Let's stand and face the danger
Squarely in the eye
Face to face and standing firm
Let the bodies pile up high

Let's not get round to lockdown
Heed my battle cry
And carry on regardless
Let the bodies pile up high

The stench of death upon my hands
May well intensify
But let's not get distracted
Let the bodies pile up high

You know me all too well by now
Could you believe that I
Could utter something heartless
Let the bodies pile up high

Oh Dominic, my Judas
Would have you crucify
For words I never ever said
Let the bodies pile up high

Let's get this in proportion
And let's not magnify
Or take it out of context
Let the bodies pile up high

The truth! The truth! What is the truth?
I'll honestly deny
The words that ever left my mouth
Let the bodies pile up high

The truth, the truth and nothing but
A barefaced shameless lie
Watch my lips – they didn't say
Let the bodies pile up high

Let the bodies pile up
Stack them up a mile up
Let the bodies pile up in their thousands way up high
Let the failures pile up
Before I tear the file up
Of everything I should have done but let it all slip by

Words Fail
#430 / 28:04:2021

I'll be honest
This is not so much of a poem
As a response

An angry response
Blood boiling and ...
Just angry

Words fail

To take to the streets
In the midst of a pandemic
Is one thing

But to appropriate
The Star of David
And make Holocaust comparisons ...

Words fail

This is not about "personal liberty"
Or "freedom of speech"
Or "the right to protest"

You are free to believe
To believe whatever you want
As am I, as are we all

You are also free to speak about it
However crackpot or conspiracy-based
But …
But

To compare yourselves with the Holocaust
Words fail
Words just fail

To have so little comprehension
So little respect for others
Zero perspective in the pursuit of your own agenda
That you stoop
Stoop
Yes, stoop so low

Words fail

Curtains For Mr Johnson
#431 / 29:04:2021

Firstly
Don't trust anyone
Who doesn't like John Lewis

Secondly
Don't trust anyone
Who doesn't know what true is

The Wheels On The Bus
#432 / 30:04:2021

The wheels on the bus are falling off
Falling off – falling off
The wheels on the bus are falling off
Day by day

The deals of the boss are turning up
Turning up – turning up
The deals of the boss are turning up
Day by day

The sleaze and the fuss is building now
Building now – building now
The sleaze and the fuss is building now
Day by day

Haiku Of Truth
#433 / 30:04:2021

"Nothing to see here"
That's correct – you seem to be
Hiding everything

All This Talk Of Decoration
While Half A World Away ...
#434 / 01:05:2021

Raging fires
Funeral pyres
Horrors still unfold
Thousands lost
Uncounted cost
Oxygen is gold

Haik-USA
#435 / 02:05:2021

I've not written much
About you recently so
Things must be better

The bar set so low
They couldn't be much worse so
Not a lot to beat

Live From Manchester
#436 / 03:05:2021

Some people are on the pitch
The players aren't

Lost The Plocht ...
Definitely
#437 / 04:05:2021

Whacht?
A royal yacht?
Two hundred million
In these times?
Surely nocht

In Other News
#438 / 05:05:2021

It was reassuring to know
That after all this time
I didn't fluff my lines
Remembered my carefully rehearsed ad libs
Timed the old poems and jokes to perfection
And even thought of two new puns

Back in school
Back in front of an audience
Doing what I do best
And loving it

X Marks The Spot
#439 / 06:05:2021

Piracy – alive and well
Money in that pot
Ill-gotten gains and raids
X marks the spot

There was a map for freedom
Seems they've lost the plot
No sense of direction
X marks the spot

Time to stand against the crimes
Time to stop the rot
Every voice is vital
X marks the spot

The pencil – mightier than the sword
On a string is all we've got
The ballot box, no treasure chest
X marks the spot

One Good Turn
#440 / 07:05:2021

Out of the blue
A man I knew
But didn't really, really know
Sent me a message on a Friday afternoon

Unexpectedly generous
This act of kindness and belief
Was affirmation and trust
He saw the potential and thought of me

A heart bigger than Manchester
One good turn
And indeed he is
Yes, one good turn preserves another

Dear Mister Starmer
#441 / 08:05:2021

You seem to have a problem
No-one knows who you really are
Or what it is you stand for
Your suit is nicer than the last one's
And your hair is neater than his
But we're not even sure how to pronounce your name

Keith ...
You seem like a nice enough chap
And sound intelligent on the telly
Especially on Prime Minister's Questions
When you speak in sentences
But we still don't know who you really are

Or what you stand for
And that's the problem
It's all a bit ... well, grey
You're all a bit grey
Labour used to be red, bright red
Working man stuff, power to the people stuff

But now you're just ... grey
And if you can't beat this shower
Then there's no hope for you
Or us either, for that matter
So Kevin – or whatever your name is
Get your act together

Otherwise we're stuck with this lot of clowns
I mean, I don't like 'em at all
But at least I know what we're getting
Or not getting
And I can trust their untrustworthiness
But you and your lot ...

Who knows?
Certainly not you eh, Keith
Just be better than them – that's all we ask

Better The Devil You Know
#442 / 09:05:2021

Aye, I know he's a bit of a devil
But at least you know
Where you stand with him, like

Yes, he tells lies
But don't they all, them lot?
It's what they do these days

At least he smiles and he's jolly
Not like the others
A bit po-faced and boring if you ask me

He's a bit of a laugh though
A bit of a lad
Wish he'd brush his hair, mind

To be honest
Don't know what the others stand for
Bit grey if truth be told

At least this new one's
Not the old one
Him? I would not trust

At all
Like I said
Better the devil you know eh?

There Is Promise In Compromise
#443 / 10:05:2021

There is a fight to be had
A battle to be won
But not with each other

First and foremost
Get rid of the real enemy
That is the job in hand

Put aside your party prejudice
Lay down your preconceptions
Accept the broad way forward

Everything else can be worked out
But first things first
Compromise is not a dirty word

Compromise is listening to all
Respecting differences
Uniting for the common good

Better to compromise with each
And win than to splinter
Disintegrate and lose again

Compromise is not a sign of weakness
But a show of strength
A position of grace

There is no moral high ground
Even though some would like to claim it
Stand on it and shout down

Compromise has promise
And that is the start
But with any compromise
The promise must be kept

What Have They Really Done For Us?
#444 / 11:05:2021

Nine new food banks in our town
N-I-N-E ... that spells nine
Labour gave us nowt like that
So the Tories get my vote this time

So ... All's Well That Ends Well ...
#445 / 12:05:2021

Hope in our hearts – the end is in sight
Once in the tunnel – we now see the light
Remember the facts
That paper the cracks
As Boris will claim that he got it all right

Something I've Been Meaning To Do
#446 / 13:05:2021

I've been meaning to write a poem
About mental health
All week
But I've had a lot on my mind
Plus there's always something else in the news
Always something else to talk about
I mean, there's lots going on
That you don't know about
But you know how it is
There's always something
That seems more important
Something to distract
Always the case
And then, when I do, like now
It's this, it's rushed
And it barely scratches the surface
We really must talk more
Sometime

The Government That's Murdering The Arts
#447 / 14:05:2021

The butchers have arrived
The abattoir's alive
This is where and how it all just starts
A rusty blade that slices
Where our cultural life is
The government that's murdering the arts

No disguising and no hiding
The slope on which we're sliding
The horses – overtaken by the carts
Values are diminished
If expression is now finished
The government that's murdering the arts

Importance is reflected
In the funding that's collected
And the funding sum is less than all the parts
The proof is in your pounds and pence
Instead of just plain common sense
The government that's murdering the arts

Difficult to put back
All of that you cut back
So don't cut back at all and leave your marks
We know your hearts aren't in it
If you're prepared to bin it
The government that's murdering the arts

This sickening decision
Of ignorant precision
A dagger blow that's straight into our hearts
The importance of the earnest
Whose purse strings are the firmest
The government that's murdering the arts

Maverick invention
Expression and intention
Must be allowed the freedom to catch sparks

Not stilting the creation
Of a future generation
The government that's murdering the arts

Almost Forgotten
#448 / 15:05:2021

It doesn't feel like it
But it is today
FA Cup Final Day

A day that was looked forward to
Special – last game of the season
The gleaming jewel on football's crown
A day when the world would stop
And dads would get their jobs done before kick off
Always three o'clock
Watching every bit of the build up
Team themed It's a Knockout
Team themed A Question of Sport
Getting excited by the sight
Of a bus on a dual carriageway stuck in traffic
Then parking at Wembley
Players in the Sunday best suits
Like a wedding stag party
Testing the pitch in shiny shoes
Seeing "The road to Wembley"
Again and again, goals on muddy pitches
All to the backing of a hastily recorded dodgy song
Picking a team to support for the day
Even though it wasn't yours
And if it was against a team you hated – even better
Yes, FA Cup Final Day was special
Not so much now
Just another match on the telly

I'll still be watching though
C'mon Leicester!
What time's kick off?

It's The Sound Of The Crowd
That Punctuates The Game
#449 / 16:05:2021

The sound of the crowd
A well-timed tackle that brings the cheers
A shot well wide that brings the jeers

The sound of the crowd
A wonder goal ignites the roars
Delirium and wild applause

The sound of the crowd
World class saves – the *oohs* and *aaahs*
The sweet relief of VAR

The sound of the crowd
Unlocked jubilation flows
As that final whistle blows

The sound of the crowd
All that pent-up shared emotion
Players' efforts, team devotion

The sound of the crowd
Players, owner – raise that cup
A city united – lifted up

"Brilliantly written poems that resonate – proud to know you."
Jayne Jones

**A Good Reason For A Hug
And A Haiku**
#450 / 17:05:2021

Today's the day I
Start my first full week of work
In over a year

There Will Be Hugs
#451 / 18:05:2021

Even though free to hug at last
I did not do so

But then again, I wasn't
Meeting old friends on a workday Monday

Random hugging of strangers
Did not seem appropriate, however legal

But I did shake hands for the first time
In a long, long time and that felt good

Those of you I know and love
And haven't seen, get ready ...

There will be hugs

I'd Forgotten How Much I Love My Job
#452 / 19:05:2021

Time fades memories
The normal changes
As new routines fall uneasily into place
Not driving the length and breadth of the country
No schools and laughter, no shows
Some things I didn't miss, some I did

And now, one week back on track
A week like "the old days"
And I'd forgotten how much I love my job
The laughter, the jokes, more laughter
But it's always about the poetry
The magic of words

A few lines from yesterday's poems
Words and ideas – not mine
But the children's …
Super-Teacher – Zoom
Flies around the room
Purple pants of course – Nursery

Summer, autumn, winter, spring
A little bit of everything
Year one – four seasons in one poem
Don't plant your pants dad
To "sisters together, sister forever" and Emmeline Pankhurst
Year two – all within forty minutes

Things to do with SATS – feed them to the fish
Flush 'em down the loo to year six memories
All in the same hour
Things we take away from here
Ibrahim in the cupboard
Scared of the snake in nursery

Every school nativity – I was always the donkey
Every school nativity – she was always the cow
The best friends we ever made

Yes, the laughter, the emotion, the connection
The magic of poetry
I'd forgotten how much I love my job

Yet
#453 / 20:05:2021

I went to the pub
For the first time in
... well, who knows

Beer, steak, football
That was the plan
I was alone, after all

Firstly, they wouldn't put my match on
Steak – good but not spectacular
Chips – passable

I thought the beer would taste better
It didn't
Was just okay

Wasn't as excited as I thought I'd be
Underwhelmed at best
Not just because I was alone

It's everyone else
Some seemed too loud, too casual
As if none of this had ever happened

I like the fact that things are opening
That I'm starting to work again
But ...

Part of me likes the caution
The consideration of others
Maybe I'm not ready for lots of other people

Yet

Great To See You John, Really Great
#454 / 21:05:2021

I don't think we'd ever hugged before
Ever
But after nearly forty years
Outside a coffee shop in the rain

We did

Not just because we could
But because it was good …
Good to see you my friend
After all this time … in these times

A great big bear hug of an embrace
And the years just slipped
We laughed, caught up
And laughed some more

Two old men talking about youth
And being an age we'd never considered
But two old friends talking about the present
And the future too

Music and connection
Songs unwritten, things still left to do
Until it was time to brave the rain once more
Another bear hug – twice in one day

A forty-year-old embrace
One thing is for sure
At our age
It won't be forty years before the next one

The Teachers Don't Talk In The Staffroom
#455 / 22:05:2021

The teachers don't talk in the staffroom
When they are all on their break
Voices are mumbling
Tummies are rumbling
Looking forward to … cake!

The teachers don't talk in the staffroom
Are they asleep or awake?
We found out why
When peeping inside …
Their mouths are full of … cake!

The teachers don't talk in the staffroom
But oh! The noises they make
Are chomping and chewing
What are they doing?
Stuffing their faces with … cake!

The teachers don't talk in the staffroom
So much time that they take …
On slices too big
They eat like a …
Gobbling lots of … cake!

The teachers don't talk in the staffroom
They all have tummy ache
Grunting and groaning
All of them moaning …
I've eaten too much … cake!

The teachers don't talk in the staffroom
But they are all putting on weight
Forgetting their diet
It's just like a riot
Racing to get to the … cake!
Chasing to get to the … cake!
Fighting to get the best … cake!

Apology Poem
#456 / 22:05:2021

Now I'm feeling guilty that today's poem
Although new to you was indeed "One I prepared earlier"
So I'm writing this – something new
Obviously it won't be as good as the one I shared
But it will be new – professional pride I suppose
Like Mastermind ... "I've started so I'll finish"
Although, to be honest, I'm not sure
If there'll ever be a finish to all this
Or the poetry

A Small Truth
#457 / 23:05:2021

Driving to my mother's
I see a sign with an arrow
Asmall CP school
Of course I read it as
A small CP school
And imagine model village scenario
But I know for a fact
That any school, however small
Always has a massive heart

What Trickery Is This
Regarding The British Weather?
#458 / 24:05:2021

What trickery is this?
Is there something that I've missed?
Something I've forgotten to remember?
The sun shone yesterday
I went to bed in May
And seem to have awoken in November

The Times, They Changed Because Of You

#459 / 25:05:2021
Bob Dylan was 80 yesterday.

One man, six strings and poetry
That chimed so clear and rang so true
Right place, right face, right voice and choice
The times they changed because of you

A genius and a joker man
Unpredictable but always new
The magic and mystique, original, unique
The times they changed because of you

Legacy in turns of phrase
A spokesman for the few
A ragged rambling rolling truth
The times they changed because of you

We can't resist the words that twist
Each simple phrase that grew and grew
Now universal language used
The times they changed because of you

Questions, riddles, answers,
All tangled up in red and blue
Foolishness and wisdom mix
The times they changed because of you

Sometime god-like reputation
A Jesus and a Judas too
Acoustic then electric, authentic then heretic
The times they changed because of you

A hurricane of chaos
A brand new wind that's blowing through
Heaven's door ajar
The times they changed because of you

The Man We Didn't Trust
Prepares To Tell Us About
The Man We Still Don't Trust
#460 / 26:05:2021

So the man behind the man
Reveals there was no plan
As we suspected all along
When all of this began

Defences at the ready
"Well, we got the big things right
Anyone can be
Professors of hindsight"

Big things – like mortality
All who didn't survive
If you'd done the little things so well
More would be alive

"So true." *Louise Dunsire*

Eleven Nights In Eccles ... And I Got No Eccles Cake
#461 / 27:05:2021

I'm back on the road again
After all this time
Eating on my own again
At the age of fifty-nine
Found coffee houses, burger bars
But here is my mistake
Eleven nights in Eccles
And no sign of a cake

When I'm here in Lancashire
My pot is always hot
And just like George I've got a little
Stick of Blackpool rock
And then I dream of Aberdeen
And a juicy Angus steak
But eleven nights in Eccles
And still no sign of cake

I've had a bun from Chelsea
I've had my Eton Mess
Worcester Sauce on my Scotch Egg
Melton Mowbray pork pies – yes!
A Bakewell tart to soothe my heart
But still I yearn and ache
Eleven nights in Eccles
And still no sign of cake

Give me a Cornish pasty
With a side of Cheddar cheese
A Yorkshire pudding stood in
A plate of Scouse but please
Just one bite of this delight
My tastebuds will awake
But eleven nights in Eccles
And still no sign of cake

No moist and spicy currants
No sugared buttered bake
I got no flaky pastry
I got no Eccles cake

Shock! Horror! Some Of Us Have Always Felt That
#462 / 28:05:2021

Once united in cahoots
The main manipulator
Now – divided chaos
The teacher has turned traitor

Once the puller of the strings
Once the chief advisor
The gloves are off, the strings are cut
Are we any wiser?

Solidarity of conspirators
No longer ever-present
It's every man for himself
As things become unpleasant

If that's the way it is with them
Then how much more with us?
Over eighties and the weak ...
Throw them underneath the bus

The bus of hollow promises
But full of death and lies
No loyalty, no morals
And sadly no surprise

So, Mister Hancock ...
#463 / 29:05:2021

"A minor breach of the rules"
The conclusion that they reach

They concentrate on "minor"
When it really should be "breach"

Respect
#464 / 30:05:2021

Second vaccination – yes
Thanks, God bless the NHS

Safer maybe – peace of mind
Relief – well, of a kind

Less risk of infection
One small step in the right direction

The longer danger hasn't passed
Still I choose to wear my mask

Mayday?
#465 / 31:05:2021

A royal yacht
Why not?
Just what we all need

Make it a priority
For that small minority
Just what we all need

The NHS is sinking
So just what are they thinking?
Just what we all need

Rather have a boat
Than keep the hospitals afloat
Just what we all need

All those bodies overboard
Are they bothered, overawed?
Just what we all need

Already been titanic
But still no need to panic
Just what we all need

Stormy seas, times like these
Still they do just as they please
Just what we all need

Cheer Up Mister Morrissey – Have A Sausage Roll
#466 / 01:06:2021

Now there's a chappy we all know
Opinionated so and so
Miserable as heaven knows – so witty and so droll
This charmless man's a real pain
His big mouth, it strikes again
Cheer up Mister Morrissey – have a sausage roll

You might say that meat is murder
Don't you beef about my burger
Bacon tofu's more absurder – like vegan toad in the hole
November spawned a Monster Munch
Every day's like Sunday lunch
Cheer up Mister Morrissey – have a sausage roll

William it was really nothing
A hot pork roll with extra stuffing
Some girls are bigger than others
Especially if they're pasty lovers
My girlfriend was in a coma
Until she sniffed that pie's aroma
Heaven knows I'm miserable now
Sheila – Sheila – take a cow

Principles you may believe in
Don't you love a fascist vegan
All hail Ayatollah Stephen – he thinks he's in control
Some might say it's heresy
To criticize his deity
But cheer up Mister Misery – have a sausage roll

Oh what difference does it make?
Just pass me that T-bone steak
You're the one for me fatty
I don't really fancy that beetroot patty
Pretty girls – they make the gravy
Shakespeare's sizzlers – oh so flavoury
I've started something I just can't finish
A bit like watching Paddy McGuinness

This joke isn't funny anymore
But at least I tried
Cheer up Mister Morrissey ...
The boy with the quorn in his side

Hopefully A Never-Ending Haiku
#467 / 02:06:2021

No-one died today
May tomorrow be the same
And the day after

Thirty Minutes – Not Much To Ask, Is It?
#468 / 03:06:2021

Thirty minutes extra on the school day
Not much to ask, is it?
It's one idea

So is having a smaller class size
Or cutting teachers' workload
Paper time, not children time obviously ...

Or not teaching fronted bastard adverbials
Or letting teachers have the flexibility
To teach the things that really matter

Or providing funds for
Sport, music, drama, the arts ...
It's time to learn to love school again

The school day doesn't need lengthening
Just needs brightening
Not much to ask, is it?

Inspired
#469 / 04:06:2021

I am reading a book
Written by my friend Michael
I've always loved his poems
But more-so now

Short lines
Of power and emotion
The fight for life
The fight for his life
In detail

Intimate, raw, honest
And funny

We have chatted since online
Mostly bad puns, jokes
And eternal football disappointment

I hope I made him smile
As much as he did me

Back to the book

My heart fills up
As I read
So do my eyes
But I am glad
That I am reading
These poems
It meant that he lived
To tell the tale

Not everyone did

A Poet, A Singer, An Artist And A Glam Rock Drummer
#470 / 05:06:2021

I used to watch Top of the Pops
Wait for Slade
And wish I was part of the band

Wanted to be a rock star
Couldn't play guitar
Or sing
Shouldn't have stopped me I know
But it did

Songs remained unsung
Potential hits unrecorded
But thanks to Roger McGough
And the Bard of Salford
Song words became poetry
So things went from bad to verse

Fast forward over forty years

Poetry returns to lyrics
For my friend Les to sing
While Martin designs logos and covers

There is a drummer too
The man all three of us watched on telly
Is our mate
And we are all in a band together

Strange how things turn out
But here we all are
Combined age of over
Two hundred and fifty

There may not be a Top of the Pops
But we do have an album
Out very soon
An actual vinyl album as well as the CD
Who'duv'thunk it bak then
When wee orl sang along but cudn't spel?

I'm Glad It Was With You
#471 / 06:06:2021
for Martyn Joseph

First live show since … well
Forever
And the lights are down

We are far enough apart
To be safe
But close enough to be together

And it feels good
No
It feels great

No bookcases
No screens
No mute buttons

Hearing the hubbub of anticipation
Looking at the waiting guitars
Whose silent silver strings will soon sing gold

There will be applause
Connection and magic
The communion of artist and audience

And so much more
Heart and empathy
Wisdom, warmth and laughter

We sang along
Relishing the opportunity
Cherishing these moments
Sharing the intimacy
Celebrating the occasion
Yearning for more nights just like this

And Martyn, my friend
Oh my soul
I'm so, so glad it was with you

Carry On Crowing
#472 / 07:06:2021

Noisy crows today
Not so much a dawn chorus
More like drone caw-ers

Maybe raucous rooks
Who knows? Either way it is
Carrion squawking

Yes, they may be black
And yes, they may be birds, but
Still they cannot sing

Stumped
#473 / 08:06:2021

Historical tweets
Racist and sexist

From a teenage cricketer
Who should have known better

Historical comments
Racist and sexist

From a Prime Minister
Who should have known better

If one is wrong
So are both

If one is in
The other shouldn't be out

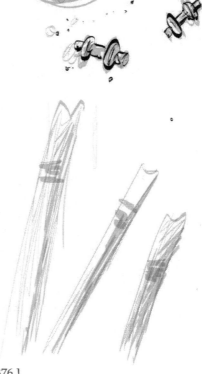

Lee Anderson And Brendan Clarke-Smith –
Thank You For Your Wisdom
#474 / 09:06:2021
All the quotes in this poem are actual quotes from the Conservative MPs
for Ashfield and Bassetlaw.

There is something wrong
Really wrong
Rotten rancid wrong
When politicians talk about
"big mistakes"
"insults to intelligence"
Being "lectured on morality"
Or "a political movement whose core principles
aim to undermine our very way of life"

Strong words indeed
But bollocks

These are footballers
United against racism
Footballers standing up to hate
Footballers saying no to monkey noises
Footballers saying we believe in equality
And taking the knee is a simple visual symbol

What do you not understand?
Or
What do you not want to understand?

These are footballers
Not politicians in a powerful party
That has consistently made "big mistakes"
Consistently "lectured on morality"
Consistently "insulted our intelligence"
And are part of a "political movement whose core principles
aim to undermine our very way of life"

With every policy that affects the poor and disadvantaged
Every food bank opened
Every school meal withheld
Every nurse undervalued
Every hospital underfunded

Every lie told
And every corrupt favour accepted

"Sick and tired of being preached and spoken down to"?
Dead right, you bet we are

"Ridiculous empty gestures"?
Well at least you know exactly
What you are talking about there
Plus National Empathy Day is tomorrow

National Empathy Day
#475 / 10:06:2021
In seven rhyming haiku verses.

I will empathise
With Tory politicians
By telling more lies

I won't take the knee
With all those other bigots
To show empathy

None of this is true
But you should always try to
See a point of view

It's empathy day
So look at situations
From another way

Don't leave out the 'a'
And 'h' for then it will be
One more empty day

If we need this day
If we have to spell it out
Things are not okay

What of tomorrow?
If we need reminding then
All this is hollow

The Value Of Truth
#476 / 11:06:2021

Truth
A commodity not valued
Or
A commodity truly valued
As
Politicians seem to be economic with it

Rafa And Novak – We Salute You
#477 / 12:06:2021

I know
I'd promised to write a football poem
Every day
Already I've failed

Apparently Italy won
And played very well indeed
But I was elsewhere

Transfixed by tennis
Hypnotised by majesty
Mesmerised by drama
Hooked on brilliance

I could not tear myself away

Just when you thought it couldn't get better
It did
Just when you thought momentum had changed
It hadn't
Just when you thought the balance of power was shifting
It wasn't
Just when you thought history would repeat
It didn't

Gladiatorial at the very least
Face to face and toe to toe
Genius outdoes genius
Again and again and again
Superlatives run dry

Artistry and grit
Sweat and toil
Spectacle and spectacular
Magnificence personified

Four hours
Four hours
Not ninety minutes
Four hours
Of blockbuster sport
Box office entertainment
And the standards never faltered

This was the court of the red clay king
And the king was dethroned
Just
Only just
Small margins
Massive victory

When the gods played for us

When Everyone Prays
For The Same Result
#478 / 13:06:2021
for Christian Eriksen

Football isn't usually a matter
Of life or death
But when it is
It is united

The Poetry Section At Waterstones
#479 / 14:06:2021

Whiling away an hour in a bookshop
Like a moth
I am drawn to poetry's flame

Not just to check if I am there
Although I always do
Even if it's just an anthology index

Children's section
Not a real section – *Fairy Tales and Gifts*
And I am invariably present

Being both egotistical and anonymous
I leave my book cover facing forward on the shelf
So the next customer sees me

Before Roald Dahl
Or Carol Ann Duffy, let's say
It makes no difference

Adult section, although copious
I am always absent
But this is no surprise

Looking first for favourites
McGough, Patten, Cooper Clarke
Ayres, Heaney and Billy Collins

I flick through pages of others
Those I'm told I should have read
Those I'm told I should be reading
Those I'm told are seminal or important
Vibrant new voices for the future
Important voices from the past

And invariably, I'm disappointed
Not because the words are not good
Just … just …

I'm yearning for something to reach out
Grab me by the heart
And say "live without me"

Something that says "buy me now"
A phrase, line, pun or joke
Wisdom I can't wait to read again

Words I want to savour
Words I can't wait to share with others
But I'm left ... wanting

Wanting more
More than this
More than these

And also knowing
That for the same price
I'd probably get one-and-a-half Stephen Kings

Instead of a slim volume
With no real cover design
And a price that puts you off even taking a chance

Still, it is indeed an hour well spent
In good company, surrounded by pages
Just waiting to find their rightful reader

Even Vera Lynn Singing Wouldn't Help
#480 / 15:06:2021

Freedom Day it isn't
So here we are again

We know one day we'll meet
Don't know where
Don't know when

Neither does Boris

Everyone For Tennis?
#481 / 16:06:2021

Everyone for Wimbledon – capacity crowd
Wembley Stadium – half allowed
Looking for consistency when socially distant
You are consistently inconsistent

So, We're All Agreed Then?
#482 / 17:06:2021

Well, it came to this?
Who would have thought it?
The country united
So, we're all agreed then
All as one
Unanimously
We are all in total agreement
With our Prime Minister
You have your Churchill moment
You have said something
No-one could possibly disagree with
Or take exception to
Unless you are, of course
Mr Hancock
Who is indeed
"Totally ****ing hopeless"
Something we all knew
And have done
For a very long time
Which begs the question ...
If that is the case
And you knew
Why didn't you do something?
Why is he still in his job?
Or is it just good
To have someone
More hopeless than yourself
To distract us all?

When Old Rivalries Renew
#483 / 18:06:2021

It's the battle of old enemies
And Euro bragging rights
Much more than just three points
And the perfect Friday night
It's the winning, it's the winning
And it doesn't matter how
Any lucky rebound counts
It's the here and it's the now
No-one wants to lose
A last gasp draw may do
In the battle of the Euros
When old rivalries renew

Form goes out the window
It's the passion on the day
The team that wants it most
Not the systems that we play
The feuding and the histories
The bitter memories
Decisions made against us
By dodgy referees
The blood and guts and bravery
The will to get us through
In the battle of the Euros
When old rivalries renew

The times we smashed it totally
The taste of victories
The times when losing we lost face
To colleagues, friends and families
Desperate to come out top
Desperate to score
Losing's not an option
We might just take a draw
And if the ball ends in the net
We really don't care who
Is the hero on the day
When old rivalries renew

The hopes we have at kick off
Reality arrives
The bitten fingernails
This rollercoaster ride
The tension, nerves, excitement
This time we'll get it right
The feeling in our water
That this time we just might
Raise our game that extra notch
So we can turn the screw
And get one over on them
When old rivalries renew

And at the end of the day
It's more than just a game
Whatever the result
Things never stay the same
We may feel over the moon
Cheer and celebrate
Or sick as dogs and parrots
As we commiserate
And there's always next time
The heart remains so true
In the duel of the year
When old rivalries renew

Great Expectations
#484 / 19:06:2021

Underperformed
Overawed
Didn't lose
At least it's a draw

Back down to earth
Usual state
Expectations
Always grate

Always A Book
#485 / 20:06:2021

In latter years
It was always a book
I can't remember what
It was when I was younger
But in the latter years
It was always a book
Invariably hardback
Seemed classier, appropriate
Often football related
Church-based or biography
Sometimes just a good story
That I know you'd read quickly

Today, I think of all the books
I haven't bought with you in mind
Although you are always in mind
Always close by, a constant barometer
I wonder what you would make of today
The modern world and its changes
Our achievements and disappointments
All the things I never got to tell you
All the football we never watched
You remembered sixty-six, never yet repeated
So today, I will reach to my bookshelf
Take down a book and open a page
You never raised an alcoholic toast
But today I raise these words to you

There was always a book with dad
And not just on Father's Day

Fifty-Six Years On
#486 / 21:06:2021

At primary school
We talked of football, football, football
Music and what we watched on the telly

Now
We still talk of football, football, football
Music, what we watched on the telly

But also
Hip replacements
Keyhole knee surgery
Heart problems and cancer
Care homes and funerals
Captaining the bowls club

And
Missed sixtieth birthday parties

**Thirty-Four Syllables Regarding Dido Harding
And Any Possible Involvement With The NHS**
#487 / 22:06:2021

When someone who has
Failed and wasted public funds
Is even thought of

We have rolled over
And you prepare to rub our
Noses in the dirt

Nots
#488 / 23:06:2021

Apparently, we should have been back to normal by now
(Whatever that may be) – but we're not

However, variant numbers on the rise and everyone thinks
It'll be okay because we have a vaccine – but it's not

And in the midst of all this confusion
Inconsistencies arise with alarming consistency
As the government seems to tie itself and then us – into knots

Every Day Is Thank A Teacher Day
#489 / 24:06:2021
for National Thank a Teacher Day

You want me to call you "Joan"
But I can't
Not really
Always Mrs Burton

Fifty years ago
(Yes, I know …)
You stood at the front of our class

Day by day
And taught us all the things
We now take for granted

We cannot remember the learning
You channelled that osmosis
On a daily basis

And all I remember
Is that it was a good time
A great time

A time of stories and writing
A time of painting and drawing
Art, craft, playing
And the collaboration of learning

Sitting by the window with Wiggy
Heatlumps, Ammo and Lewo
Always close by
A time we all enjoyed

We must have done grammar
But not like today
Thank goodness

And here we are
Fifty years later
(Yes, I know ...)
All still here

And you, still commenting on my poems
Not marking them
But telling me it's the best homework
I've ever done

And me, still relishing those comments
Loving the fact that you love these poems

Even though I can call you "Joan"
I still think Mrs Burton
I still thank Mrs Burton
Thank you

Joan

No Weddings, More Funerals
#490 / 25:06:2021

Not a good title for a comedy film
But we are getting to that stage
That uncertain age
Everyday aches and pains
Conditions our grandparents complained of
Health we once took for granted
Where an unexpected telephone call
Or email out of the blue
Is often news we rather we didn't have to hear
Failing health, sudden illnesses
Hospital visits and operations
Cancer conversations seem regular these days
Closer to the end than the beginning
Not every story has a happy ending
That uncertain age

Clear As Mud
#491 / 25:06:2021

You can watch the fastest racing cars
But not those who play guitars

Watch and cheer a winning goal
But you can't rock and you can't roll

See the horses, race and bet
Theatres ain't seen nothing yet

It's everyone for tennis
But gigs ... who knows when is

The time for all these rules to change
Treat everybody just the same

Instead, as usual, we discover
One rule for some, one rule for others

**At No Point Will This Poem Descend Into Cheap Puns Regarding
The Unfortunate Nature Of His Surname And The Current
Situation He Finds Himself In Which Is Obviously A Private Matter**
#492 / 26:06:2021

If he can do it, nothing to it – a snog and then a grope
The man who was hopeless is giving all men hope
Now we know why track and trace didn't have a clue
When Mrs H couldn't find a track and trace on you

Hands, face, space – just what could it mean?
Your hands – her face – no space in between
Two metres apart – not your way of life
Until you get home – much more with your wife

Stay home – save lives – advice that you have known
Not sure that's the case when you go home
You might meet matrimonial resistance
You're going to find the real meaning of social distance

Lies and deception – nothing really sinister
Just in training to be the next Prime Minister
Horror! Surprise! Revulsion! Shock!
The two go together – Matt and Cock

I know the title said I wouldn't sink as low as that
But I was telling lies – just like Matt
Cheap and puerile, perhaps I'd better stop
The two go together – Matt and Cock

That's below the belt – a real cheap shot
Just like Matt – just like his …

A Message On Behalf Of The Prime Minister
#493 / 27:06:2021

I just want you to know   You may ask me why
That I always backed him   Just how can that be
His job was always safe   Well, it's good to have someone
I would not have sacked him   Who's a bigger pratt than me

[391]

Papers At A Bus Stop In A Random Street In Kent
#494 / 28:06:2021

We all believe in freedom – and freedom of speech
Freedom of information – but security's been breached
Just how could it happen? What was the intent
With papers at a bus stop in a random street in Kent?

Soggy, strewn and sensitive – and not for prying eyes
The governmental density that nothing can disguise
Secrecy and service – just not evident
With papers at a bus stop in a random street in Kent

What's the plan? Afghanistan? Maybe the Black Sea
The rushing of the Russians against our MOD
Not much of a plan that they try to implement
With papers at a bus stop in a random street in Kent

Possible manoeuvres for HMS Defender
No papers marked with "please return to sender"
But the BBC and licence fee – money that's well spent
For papers at a bus stop in a random street in Kent

So who lives in Kent? Who travels on a bus?
Shouldn't be that hard to find – who caused all the fuss
So what are the excuses that they're trying to invent
For the papers at a bus stop in a random street in Kent

But procedures are in place – hoping to ensure
That this sort of accident won't happen any more
Going to stop the problem – this is what they meant
They're going to take away all the bus stops there in Kent

Dear Gareth ... Dear England
#495 / 29:06:2021

You have a unique opportunity
You carry the hopes and dreams of a nation

May they lift you and give you feet of fire
May they free you to play with risk and reward
May they inspire you to greater things
And may the spirit inside burn brighter, stronger, longer

Do not be afraid of history
Do not be weighed down by doubt
Do not be shackled by negativity
Do not be held back for fear of falling

In any match
One team must lose
And one team must win
That is how it always is
But that is what excites us
Jeopardy and opportunity – hand in hand
Success and failure – both within our grasp

Already this will be a lifelong memory
Already this will be a snapshot
A pivotal moment that we experience together

But you have the chance to make it special
Really special
You have the chance to be immortal
You have the chance to be heroes
The chance to be legends

You are doing what we could only dream of
What most of us have dreamed of
So make those dreams come true
And win

Win for us
Win for England

Or

Lose – but if that is the way it must be
Then lose by being brave
Run till you can run no more
Put your bodies on that line
Dig deep
Then deeper still
Do not leave that field of dreams
With anything left to give
With anything you should have done

Just make us proud
Then make us prouder still

Let the lions roar
Until they can roar no more

Do this and we shall remember this moment forever

Dear Gareth – dear England
History awaits

Thank You
#496 / 30:06:2021

Thank you Gareth and Raheem
Thank you Harry, thank you team

Ghosts are vanquished, curses lifted
Hoodoo banished, demons dealt with

A nation breathes, a nation sighs
Fires kindle, hopes arise

Celebration and relief
Realisation and belief

Thank you England, thank you team
Dare we hope, dare we dream ...

Not Clever, Not Witty, Just Stupid
#497 / 01:07:2021

Protestors protesting
About the freedom to believe
What they think is the truth
Harass a man
Who has the freedom to believe
What he thinks is the truth

Louder Than You
#498 / 02:07:2021

Well, you shout about the empire
You shout about the flag
You shout for Queen and country
And the greatness we once had
You shout about our history
But not about today
Yes, you who shout the loudest
Have nothing much to say

You shout about the football
About the price of beer
You shout about the refugees
Escaping over here
You're full of smoke and mirrors
It's hot air and it's gas
Cos you who shout the loudest
Are talking through your ass

Silence may be golden
But it's time now to be loud
Time to raise our voices
And shout above the crowd
For those who raise their voices
Are those who dare to doubt
All you who shout the loudest
With the least to shout about

We're going to shout it loud and proud
Together, trusted, true
Shout it louder till we are
Louder than you

Shout out every single truth
Every single word
Carry on our shouting
Till our voices can be heard
From the rising of the sun
To the shining of the moon
We'll shout while we are dancing
To a different freedom tune

We're going to shout for justice
We're going to shout for peace
Equality not poverty
Resolution and release
Shout that lives all matter
Until our throats are raw
And when you think we're beaten …
Then we'll shout a little more!

And

Drown out your distraction
Drown out all your lies
Drown your pointless waffle
And needless compromise
Drown out your intolerance
These fires that you stoke
Drown your bigotry with love
And drown your hate with hope

We're going to shout it loud and proud
Shout it once again
Just remember this
Hate won't win

Heads We Win, Tails You Lose
#499 / 03:07:2021

Wimbledon and Wembley, a myriad smiling faces
Parents who cannot attend their children's sports day races

Two sides of the coin – one a win and one a loss
I suppose it all depends on just who gives a toss

Poem Five Hundred
#500 / 04:07:2021

Poem five hundred – in less than two years
Daily undertaking, creative exercise

Writing routinely – but not routinely writing
A habit formed I don't want to break

Surprising myself – loving the challenge
Some things I knew, something that's new

All these poems – I would never have written
All these words, asleep, undisturbed

Each day I wake – shake them all up
Each day they fall, find their own shape

Each poem a journey – new and exciting
Less than two years, five hundred poems

"When we look back at 2020/21 and think *'what was all that about?'*, his work will help us to remember and to see how far we've come."
Rev. Kate Bottley

flapjackpress.co.uk